STUDENT UNIT GUIDE

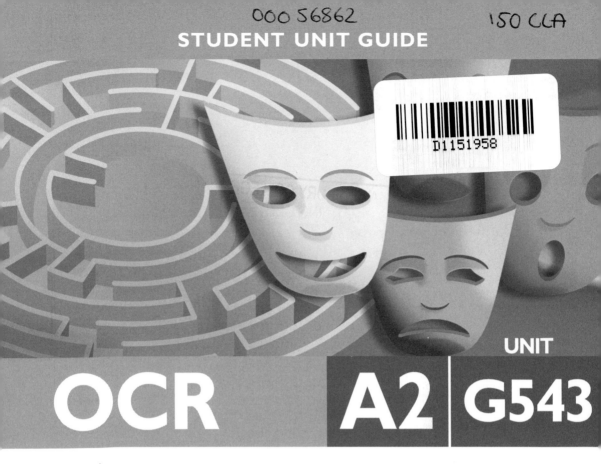

OCR | A2 | UNIT G543

Psychology

Health and Clinical Psychology

David Clarke

Philip Allan Updates, an imprint of Hodder Education, an Hachette UK company, Market Place, Deddington, Oxfordshire OX15 0SE

Orders

Bookpoint Ltd, 130 Milton Park, Abingdon, Oxfordshire OX14 4SB
tel: 01235 827720
fax: 01235 400454
e-mail: uk.orders@bookpoint.co.uk

Lines are open 9.00 a.m.–5.00 p.m., Monday to Saturday, with a 24-hour message answering service. You can also order through the Philip Allan Updates website: www.philipallan.co.uk

© Philip Allan Updates 2008

ISBN 978-0-340-97615-9

First printed 2009
Impression number 5 4 3
Year   2014 2013 2012 2011 2010

This guide has been written specifically to support students preparing for the OCR A2 Psychology Unit G543 examination. The content has been neither approved nor endorsed by OCR and remains the sole responsibility of the author.

Typeset by Phoenix Photosetting, Chatham, Kent
Printed by MPG Books, Bodmin

Hachette UK's policy is to use papers that are natural, renewable and recyclable products and made from wood grown in sustainable forests. The logging and manufacturing processes are expected to conform to the environmental regulations of the country of origin.

Contents

Introduction

■ ■ ■

Content Guidance

■ ■ ■

Questions & Answers

Introduction

About this guide

This book is a guide to the **Health and Clinical Psychology** option of **Unit G543** of the new OCR A2 specification (aggregation code H568). It is not a textbook, but it is an aid to help you through the course and your revision. The emphasis is on informing you of exactly what you need to do and what you need to know to be successful in the examinations.

This guide has three sections:
- **Introduction.** This outlines the specification requirements for the Health and Clinical Psychology option. It discusses the background to the course and the topic areas. It also includes guidance on what to study, assessment objectives and a useful section on how to evaluate.
- **Content Guidance.** This takes you through the material that you need to cover for the examinations. Fundamental to all psychology courses are the central approaches of psychology, which are cognitive psychology, developmental psychology, social psychology, physiological psychology and the psychology of individual differences. It also gives details of the methods used for health and clinical psychology along with issues and perspectives that run through the course. Many marks can be gained from a simple evaluation strategy, so this section helps you to develop your own evaluative skills, and therefore get a better grade.
- **Questions and Answers.** The answers provided here are not intended to be model answers, so don't learn them and try to reproduce them in your own examination. The best thing to do is to look at the responses and the examiner's comments and then try and apply the best techniques to your own answers. You might find it useful to attempt your own answer to the specimen questions before you read the examiner's comments.

Background

The fundamental questions of psychology are:
- Why do I behave like this?
- Why do I feel like this?
- Why do I think like this?

There is no denying that these are *big* questions, and it is worth keeping them in the back of your mind when you are looking at the evidence in health and clinical psychology.

The examiners say that this specification encourages students to:
- consider the big questions

- evaluate the evidence
- have an opinion

In other words, you do not have to learn what everyone else says and agree with whatever they say. What you must do is look at the evidence and figure out your own opinions — this is the route to success on this course. Don't keep learning more and more information, but be sure of what you do know and be prepared to comment on it.

The key questions for students to consider when studying A2 options in psychology are:

- What are the key terms and concepts?
- What is the psychological evidence?
- What can we say about the quality of this evidence?
- How can we apply this evidence?

There are also some supplementary questions to consider, including:

- How does health and clinical psychology relate to the themes and issues?
- How does health and clinical psychology relate to the five core approaches?
- How does health and clinical psychology use different methods?

The questions in this unit refer specifically to the psychology of health, and include:

- Why do people not adhere to medical requests?
- How can we encourage people to take better care of their health?
- What causes stress, and how can we reduce stress?
- What is dysfunctional behaviour: how is it explained?
- What is a mental disorder, and how can it be treated?

When you look at these questions, you will soon guess that there is no simple answer to any of them. (In fact, there is probably not even one 'complicated' answer.)

So, while you are not expected to come up with solutions to these problems, you are required to:

- *Describe* some theories, studies and evidence that are relevant to the question.
- *Evaluate* those theories, studies and evidence that are relevant to the question.
- *Apply* the methods, perspectives and issues relevant to health and clinical psychology.
- *Apply* health and clinical psychology to real-life events and situations.

The A2 specification

Skills from AS

The options in applied psychology build on the work you have done in the AS part of the course in a number of ways:

- How the five core approaches of psychology — cognitive psychology, develop-mental psychology, social psychology, physiological psychology and the psychology of individual differences — apply in a variety of real-world contexts.
- How the range of methods and techniques covered at AS (self-report, experiments, observations and correlation) are also used in each of the A2 options.
- How the methodological issues, such as reliability and validity, sampling techniques, experimental designs and data-analysis techniques appear in each of the A2 options.
- How psychological issues, debates and perspectives raised at AS — such as ethics, ecological validity, quantitative and qualitative data and snapshot and longitu-dinal studies — apply with just as much frequency in each of the A2 options.

New skills for A2

The A2 course introduces a number of new debates that are not covered at AS. These debates are:
- determinism and free will
- reductionism and holism
- nature–nurture
- ethnocentrism
- psychology as a science
- individual and situational explanations
- the usefulness of psychological research

Each of these debates are looked at in more detail in the Content Guidance section.

The OCR topic areas

Healthy living
There are many factors that influence our healthy lifestyles. These can include our beliefs about health and how healthy behaviour is promoted. An example of healthy behaviour is adherence to medical advice.

Theories of health belief
- health belief model (e.g. Feshbeck)
- locus of control (e.g. Rotter)
- self-efficacy (e.g. Bandura)

Methods of health promotion and supporting evidence
- media campaign (e.g. Cowpe 1989)
- legislation (e.g. Dannenberg 1993)
- fear arousal (e.g. Janis and Feshbeck 1953)

Features of adherence to medical regimes and supporting evidence
- reasons for non-adherence: cognitive rational non-adherence (e.g. Bulpitt)
- measures of non-adherence: physiological (e.g. Lustman 2000)
- improving — behavioural (e.g. Watt's funhaler 2003)

Stress

Stress appears to be a major factor in the health of people, with psychologists interested in improving the health of the nation by identifying causes, and trying to encourage stress-management techniques

Causes of stress and supporting evidence
- work (e.g. Johansson et al. 1978)
- hassles and life events (e.g. Kanner 1981)
- lack of control (e.g. Geer and Maisel 1973)

Methods of measuring stress and supporting evidence
- physiological measures (e.g. Geer and Maisel 1973)
- self-report (e.g. Holmes and Rahe 1967)
- combined approach (e.g. Johansson et al. 1978)

Techniques for managing stress and supporting evidence
- cognitive (e.g. SIT, Meichenbaum 1977, 1984)
- behavioural (e.g. biofeedback, Budzynski 1970)
- social (e.g. social support, Waxler-Morrison 1991)

Dysfunctional behaviour

Dysfunctional behaviour is atypical behaviour psychologists are interested in explaining and treating, whichever psychological approach is adopted.

Diagnosis of dysfunctional behaviour
- categorising (e.g. DSM/ICD)
- definitions (e.g. Rosenhan and Seligman 1989)
- biases in diagnosis (e.g. gender; Ford and Widiger 1989)

Explanations of dysfunctional behaviour
- biological (e.g. genetic; Gottesman and Shields 1972; Ost 1992)
- behavioural (e.g. classical conditioning; little Albert 1920; Lewinsohn 1979)
- cognitive (e.g. maladaptive thoughts, Beck 1979; DiNardo 1988; Seligman 1979)

Treatments of dysfunctional behaviour
- biological (e.g. SRRIs; Karp and Frank 1995)
- behavioural (e.g. desensitisation; Wolpe 1958; McGrath 1990)
- cognitive (e.g. cognitive therapy; Beck 1979; Dobson 1989)

Disorders

This option introduces the different types of disorder, such as anxiety, affective and psychotic, their characteristics, causes and treatments.

Characteristics of disorders
- an anxiety disorder (e.g. phobia)
- a psychotic disorder (e.g. schizophrenia)
- an affective disorder (e.g. bipolar)

Explanations of one disorder (affective, anxiety or psychotic)

- behavioural (e.g. classical conditioning, Watson and Raynor; Lewinsohn 1979 for affective)
- biological (e.g. genetic psychotic, Gottesman and Shields 1972, genetic affective Oruc et al. 1998)
- cognitive (e.g. DiNardo 1998 for anxiety, Seligman 1979 for affective)

Treatments for one disorder (affective, anxiety or psychotic)

- behavioural (desensitisation, Wolpe; Paul and Lentz 1977 for psychotic, McGrath 1990 for anxiety)
- cognitive behavioural therapy (e.g. RET; Ellis, Comer 1998 for affective, Ost and Westling 1995 for anxiety, Sensky 2000 for psychotic)
- biological (e.g. drugs, biochemical; Karp and Frank 1995 for affective, Comer 1998 for psychotic)

Examination guidance

The G543 *Options in Applied Psychology* examination paper lasts for 1½ hours and the format is as follows:

Answer **four** questions in total; **two** questions from **two** options only. Put another way, you must answer **two** questions from **one** option (health and clinical psychology) and **two** questions from another option (forensic **or** sport **or** education).

All four options will appear on the same examination paper. Never answer questions from an option that you have not studied. Do not even read the questions from the options you have not studied.

The question format for each paper is exactly the same:
- **(a)** Describe or Outline, which carries 10 marks.
- **(b)** Evaluate, Assess, Discuss or Review, which carries 15 marks.

You have 45 minutes to answer questions from the health and clinical option (and 45 minutes to answer questions from your second chosen option). The examination paper therefore lasts for 90 minutes.

Question part (a) will always ask you to 'describe' or 'outline'. To outline means exactly the same as describe. In theory, an outline question should be shorter than a description, but in reality you get exactly the same amount of time and you need to write just as much, so there is no difference between the two. Describing is an AO1 skill, so do not evaluate in question part (a) as it will score no marks.

Question part (b) will always ask you to 'discuss' or 'evaluate' or 'assess' or 'review'. All of these require you to comment on what is good and what is not so good — to give positives and negatives and, if you can, to compare and to contrast evidence. Discussing is an AO2 skill, so do not describe in question part (b) unless you introduce new evidence, and if you do, then make your description brief and to the point.

Candidates often finish writing ahead of time. However, there is no prize for finishing first, and candidates who finish early will probably not do as well as they expect. Which candidate are you? Are you the one who finishes early or do you give that little bit more detail, guaranteeing that you achieve a maximum mark for each question?

On the other hand, whatever you do, don't run out of time. Be strict with yourself. Try testing yourself so that you know exactly how much you can write in the time allowed. Ask your teacher to give you test essays on examination questions.

The table below summarises the mark allocation, time allocation, and recommended length of answer for the Health and Clinical option only. The same format is repeated for your second chosen option.

	Mark allocation	Time spent on question	Amount of writing
First question part (a)	10 marks	8 min	½ side A4
First question part (b)	15 marks	14 min	1 side A4
Second question part (a)	10 marks	8 min	½ side A4
Second question part (b)	15 marks	14 min	1 side A4
Totals	**50 marks**	**44 min**	**3 sides A4**

Note that if you can write more than the amount suggested, you should do so.

Assessment objectives

You do not need to worry too much about the details of assessment objectives. When the examiners set exam papers, they follow the specification guidelines and include a certain percentage of each assessment objective. The wording of each question must make it clear which assessment objective is being assessed. For example, some questions ask you to describe and others ask you to evaluate. So, all you have to do is answer the questions that are set. The skills covered by each assessment objective are summarised below.

Assessment objective 1: knowledge and understanding
You should be able to:
- recognise, recall and show understanding of scientific knowledge
- select, organise and communicate relevant information in a variety of forms, including extended prose

AO1 assesses what you know about psychology and whether you understand what you know. Examination questions here would ask you to outline or describe.

Assessment objective 2: application of knowledge and understanding

You should be able to:

- analyse and evaluate scientific knowledge when presenting arguments and ideas
- apply scientific knowledge to unfamiliar situations including those related to issues
- assess the validity, reliability and credibility of scientific information
- bring together and apply scientific knowledge from different areas of the subject

AO2 assesses your evaluation skills and examination questions would ask you to discuss, evaluate or assess.

Assessment objective 3: science in practice

You should be able to:

- demonstrate ethical, safe and skilful practical techniques, selecting appropriate qualitative and quantitative methods
- make and record reliable and valid observations and measurements with appropriate precision and accuracy
- analyse, interpret, explain and evaluate the results of experimental and investigative activities in a variety of ways

There is no AO3 assessed in the Health and Clinical option, or any other option in Applied Psychology. AO3 is assessed as part of Psychological Investigations and Approaches and Research Methods in Psychology.

Mark schemes

OCR has simplified mark schemes that apply across each option paper and the same mark scheme applies to every question you will answer. This means that you only ever need to be familiar with one mark scheme, whatever question you choose and whichever option you are doing.

For question part (a), in order to achieve a mark in the top band:

- *Psychological terminology* must be used accurately.
- *Description* must be relevant, accurate, coherent and detailed.
- *Elaboration* — the interpretation/explanation of evidence and use of examples must be good.
- *Structure* of your answer must be competent and well organised
- *Grammar and spelling* must be as perfect as it can be.

For question part (b), in order to achieve a mark in the top band:

- *Evaluative points* — there must be many, covering a range of issues.
- *Argument* must be balanced, organised and well developed.
- *Examples* must be used effectively.
- *Analysis*: the drawing of valid conclusions, the summarising of issues and the construction of arguments must be highly skilled.
- *Understanding* must be shown throughout the answer.
- The answer must be explicitly related to the context of the question.

How to evaluate

Evaluation can sometimes appear to be the most difficult part of any course but it need not be. You may have heard your teacher talking about assessment objective AO2 but you may be unsure what it is. If you have an opinion and can justify it, then you can evaluate. If you say 'I think that's rubbish' then it is abuse rather than evaluation.

However, if you say 'I think it's rubbish because' and add appropriate comment then you are evaluating. Evaluation also takes into account what is good and gives credit where it is due. The OCR philosophy has always been to credit answers where students show they can think. For instance, if study X has been performed in a laboratory then you do not need to study a textbook and conclude 'A.N. Other writes that study X is low in ecological validity because it was performed in a laboratory', as you can conclude this for yourself.

How to construct an argument

You will notice from above that the question part (b) mark scheme includes comments about the quality of your argument. To get into the top band, your argument must be 'competently organised, balanced and well developed'. In addition, the argument should be 'highly skilled' and show 'thorough understanding'. So what does an argument like this look like?

If you have studied critical thinking, you will know that an argument in its simplest form looks like this:

Claim	The samples used by researchers in the fear arousal study lack generalisability.
Reason	This is because the researchers used opportunity samples of students to carry out the research.
Conclusion	Therefore, we should be cautious when applying the findings from students to actual fear arousal.

Some of you may have learned to construct your argument using the 'point example comment' (PEC) method, which can be applied to the above structure, or you may have used PEE (Point, example, explain the first two) with your work. This will give your answer a basic structure that will be easy for an examiner to follow, but it would not meet the top band criteria of being 'well developed' and 'demonstrating thorough understanding'. So how do you do this?

First, consider how much stronger your argument would be if you used evidence as well as reason to support your claim. So in our example:

Claim	The samples used by researchers in the fear arousal study lack generalisability.
Reason	This is because the researchers used opportunity samples of students to carry out the research.
Evidence	Janis and Feshback used psychology students to carry out their research into fear arousal and oral hygiene.
Conclusion	Therefore, we should be cautious when applying the findings from students to actual fear arousal.

Now go one step further. Add evaluative comment to the evidence quoted.

Claim	The samples used by researchers in the fear arousal study lack generalisability.
Reason	This is because the researchers used opportunity samples of students to carry out the research.
Evidence	Janis and Feshback used psychology students to carry out their research into fear arousal and oral hygiene.
Evaluative comment	The problem with this is that psychology students who are getting credit for their degrees by taking part are likely to show uncharacteristic behaviour by perhaps being more willing to give the researchers the findings they want. This is because they will be familiar with fear arousal from their own reading and may be tuned in to any cues the researcher may unconsciously give and also more likely to guess the researcher's aim. This is called showing demand characteristics.
Conclusion	Therefore, we should be cautious when applying the findings from students to actual fear arousal.

If you wanted to be really thorough in demonstrating your understanding, you could go even further and add a counter-comment or argument. This would look like:

Claim	The samples used by researchers in the fear arousal study lack generalisability.
Reason	This is because the researchers used opportunity samples of students to carry out the research.
Evidence	Janis and Feshback used psychology students to carry out their research into fear arousal and oral hygiene.

Evaluative comment	The problem with this is that psychology students who are getting credit for their degrees by taking part are likely to show uncharacteristic behaviour by perhaps being more willing to give the researchers the findings they want. This is because they will be familiar with fear arousal from their own reading and may be tuned in to any cues the researcher may unconsciously give and also more likely to guess the researcher's aim. This is called showing demand characteristics.
Counter-comment	On the other hand, Janis and Feshback need the convenience of an opportunity sample to be able to complete their research in a reasonable time and against a limited budget. Also, from this initial research other studies could be done using different participants and a different topic area.
Conclusion	Therefore, we should be cautious when applying the findings from students to actual fear arousal.

There are many other ways this same claim or point could have been explained but the example above shows you how an argument can be developed to demonstrate understanding.

Content
Guidance

This section looks in more detail at the OCR specification, the core approaches, perspectives, issues and methods that relate to health and clinical psychology. The question is how the approaches, perspectives, issues and methods can be integrated to arrive at the best explanation for our health behaviour.

The four sections of the specification are:

- **Healthy living**
- **Stress**
- **Dysfunctional behaviour**
- **Disorders**

There are five core *approaches* of psychology:

- **Cognitive**
- **Developmental**
- **Physiological**
- **Social**
- **Individual differences**

There are two *perspectives*:

- **Behavioural**
- **Psychodynamic**

There are a number of *debates and issues*:

- **Ethics**
- **Ecological validity**
- **Longitudinal and snapshot studies**
- **Qualitative data and quantitative data**
- **Determinism and free will**
- **Reductionism and holism**
- **Nature–nurture**
- **Ethnocentrism**
- **Psychology as a science**
- **Individual and situational explanations**
- **The usefulness of psychological research**

There are four main *methods*:

- **Experimental**
- **Case studies**
- **Self-reports**
- **Observations**

Health psychology: healthy living

Theories of health belief

This section looks at healthy (or unhealthy) lifestyles and raises questions about the underlying reasons for lifestyle behaviours. Simply, what determines our attitudes, cognitions and behaviours in relation to our lifestyle? There are three main aspects to this:

(1) What determines our **beliefs** towards our lifestyle?
(2) How much **control** over our lifestyle do we think we have?
(3) To what extent are we **competent** to change our lifestyle?

The first of these aspects is explained by health belief models, the second by Rotter's locus of control and the third by Bandura's self-efficacy theory.

Health belief models

There are a number of health belief models that try to explain why we think and behave the way we do in relation to our health. The classic is the health belief model proposed by Becker and Rosenstock (1984). Central to this model is **perceived seriousness** and **perceived susceptibility** — our assessment of how serious an illness or lifestyle behaviour is, and how likely we are to get it. So, if we perceive an illness to be serious and that we are susceptible to it, then we may change our lifestyle to reduce the chances of us getting this illness. But, if our perception is that it *isn't* serious and that we are *not* susceptible, then we will not change our views or our behaviour. We will also do nothing if we perceive that it is serious but that we are not susceptible. For example, even if all people perceive that cancer is serious, do all people perceive that they are susceptible?

This brings in a series of further aspects to this model known as **perceptions and modifying factors**. This involves factors such as age, sex and personality, which influence our perceived susceptibility. So if you are a 17-year-old and female you will have the belief that you are not susceptible to testicular cancer, and so your behaviour will not change. But, if you are a 17-year-old male, then you are susceptible to testicular cancer, because it is the largest cause for cancer deaths among 16–35 year olds. This means that you should be performing testicular self-examination regularly, and by doing this you are changing your lifestyle because of your health beliefs. But, if you are male, you might decide not to self-examine because your personality may tell you that 'it won't happen to you', because you have **optimistic bias**. Optimistic bias is the main reason why many people continue to smoke cigarettes even though they cause lung and many other cancers: people falsely believe that it won't happen to them. So any male reading this section: did you know that you were susceptible to testicular cancer? If you didn't, then another aspect to this health belief model has just been introduced: **cues to action**. This simply means that something has prompted you and you have become aware of new information that you need to think about.

Even though you might perceive testicular cancer to be serious, that you are susceptible to it (because of your sex, age etc.) you still may not do anything about it, such as self-examine. Why not? The final part of this health belief model is that we perform an assessment of the **perceived barriers against the perceived benefits**. In other words we do a cost–benefit analysis looking at whether the perceived benefits of changing our behaviour will be greater than the perceived barriers. If all 17-year-old males self-examine their testicles, then early detection would have a definite benefit in relation to successful treatment. Even after reading this, many males will still not self-examine because of other perceptions and modifying factors, or perceived barriers.

Locus of control

Any health belief model tries to explain the factors that make up our views towards our lifestyles. But perhaps there is an alternative determinant of our lifestyle behaviour. Do we believe that we are in control of our lifestyle and if we take action we will be healthy and if we don't we won't? Alternatively, do we think that if we are going to get ill then we will and so there is no point in trying to live a healthy lifestyle, because we cannot prevent illness and have no control over it at all?

In 1966 Rotter outlined the concept of locus of control. Rotter believed that we either have an **internal locus of control**, which means that we believe *we have control* over events and forces that determine our lives, or we have an **external locus of control**, which means that we believe our life is controlled by external forces and events and that *we have very little or no control* over these forces.

This model is often applied in education: if people have an internal locus of control then they believe that they can achieve a grade A* if they have a mind to do so. In health it means that if they become ill, then they can control it, beat it and survive. Many studies have shown that people who 'beat' cancer are those with an internal locus of control.

Self-efficacy

In 1977 Bandura proposed the concept of **self-efficacy**. This is our belief about how we can perform in a particular situation, and our competence about this will affect our attitudes, cognitions and behaviours. In relation to health, if we believe that we are able to act successfully then we are more likely to put effort into an action because we believe it will be successful. On the other hand, if we do not believe we will be successful then we believe that there is no point in trying. Ask yourself: could you run the London marathon? If you are not an athlete, then you may immediately decide that you cannot, but if you were an athlete, you would take other factors into account. We decide on our level of competence or self-efficacy because of how we perform in other aspects of life and also because of the following:

- **Observations of the performance of others:** 'If he/she can do it then so can I.'
- **Social and self-persuasion:** 'I know I can do it if I try my hardest.'
- **Monitoring our emotional states:** 'I can't do it today; I'm too tired or not in the mood.'

These factors may influence your decision to run the marathon or not. What about your health behaviour? What about quitting smoking? What about dieting success-fully? Your competence to achieve a goal will be determined by your level of self-efficacy.

Methods of health promotion

There are two main ways through which health can be promoted: by **providing infor-mation** and by **arousing fear**. Such methods can be implemented in a number of ways: via **media campaigns** for example, and health promotion campaigns can be conducted in schools, worksites and whole communities. Governments can also intro-duce **legislation** to force people to change their lifestyle behaviour. The OCR speci-fication focuses on a media campaign, government legislation and the fear arousal method.

Media campaigns

A successful television media campaign was on the dangers of chip-pan fires. Cowpe (1989) reported on how the Wales/West and North East television regions of the UK received the 12-week campaign. The strength of the campaign lay in the use of both providing information and fear arousal. One television advert was presented by a woman who told of the dangers of a chip-pan fire and then in three simple steps what to do should a fire break out. However, in her case she had not followed these steps and had been burned in a chip-pan fire; the advert showed a close-up of her disfig-urement. The success of the campaign was then measured through actual fire brigade statistics. During the campaign one television region saw a 32% reduction in the number of fires, and in the 25 weeks after the campaign, although the reduction in the number of fires did decrease, it was still 17% less than before the start of the campaign. Up to a year after the campaign had started, there was still an 8% reduc-tion from baseline. This study recorded objective data in the form of fire brigade statistics. Its effectiveness over time could be assessed and it showed the need for any health-promotion campaign to be repeated periodically. There have been other television advertising campaigns, such as that reported by McVey and Stapleton (2000), which used actor John Cleese to arouse fear in smokers.

Legislation

Whereas media campaigns can induce people to change to a healthier lifestyle, one way to ensure that people do in fact live a healthier lifestyle is to change the law. Changing the law can force them to adhere to a particular behaviour. While a government cannot make it law that people eat more healthily, it can restrict where people smoke and it can make it law that people — particularly children — wear cycle helmets. While the compulsory wearing of cycle helmets has not yet become law in the UK, it has in Maryland in the USA. In Howard County, pre-law helmet use was 4%, rising to 47% post-law. It is claimed that this is the highest documented for all US children. While not everyone adheres to a law (some people still drink and drive, for example) adherence will cut deaths and injuries significantly. In the Maryland study it is claimed that wearing helmets will prevent 100 deaths and 56,000 hospitalised head injuries each year.

Fear arousal

The idea here is that fear can be aroused in people by suggesting to them what might happen if they do not change their behaviour. The UK government has run several successful fear-arousing television campaigns to target particular behaviours, such as speeding, the wearing of seat-belts and drink-driving.

The classic study in this area is by Janis and Feshback (1953). They studied fear arousal applied to oral hygiene in students. There were four groups: (i) a minimal fear group, (ii) a moderate fear group, (iii) a strong fear group and (iv) a control group. They assessed effectiveness of each level of fear through self-report questionnaires given before, immediately after and 1 week after the fear presentations. It was found that although the strong fear group did arouse most fear, the minimal fear presentation was most effective in conformity to oral hygiene behaviour.

Other studies have used the fear arousal technique such as that by Leventhal, Pagano and Watts (1967) on smokers and Thornton et al. (2000) in an anti-speeding campaign.

There are several interesting debates around the concept of fear arousal:
- Whether a high fear level is more effective than a middle or lower level of fear and various studies provide contradictory evidence. Compare the Janis and Feshback study with that of Leventhal et al. (1967), who found that high fear arousal was more effective.
- The extent to which it is ethical to scare people. While arousing fear may well be considered to be unethical to many, there is the counter-view it is worthwhile if people stop drink-driving or give up smoking. If they give up such behaviours perhaps the ends have justified the means.

Features of adherence to medical regimes

Reasons for non-adherence

People often do not arrive for medical appointments, they do not follow treatment programmes and they frequently do not take their medicine. But *why* do people not adhere to medical requests? People do not do what a medical practitioner tells them to for a variety of reasons. One explanation is that the barriers against taking medicine may be greater than the benefits of taking it, as explained by the health belief model. A different explanation is that people simply believe that it is not in their best interests to continue taking the medicine, so they stop. People take medicine initially because they feel ill, but after a few days they begin to feel well again, so they stop taking their medicine. Doctors do not prescribe surplus medicine that can be saved for later — all the medicine must be taken to totally eradicate the illness. However, if people feel better they have a rational explanation for not continuing to take the medicine.

One study to illustrate rational non-adherence is that by Bulpitt (1998). Male participants were taking a new medicine for hypertension. While the drug did reduce the number of headaches and the extent of their depression compared to pre-drug states, on the negative side, the men experienced more problems with ejaculation and impotence. Given such side effects many of the men made the rational decision to stop taking the medicine.

Measures of non-adherence

Non-adherence to medical requests can be measured in many ways. There are subjective measures, often using qualitative data, which include asking the medical practitioner, the patient or the patient's family about the extent of the patient's adherence. However, these types of measure can be influenced by demand characteristics, social desirability or simply the fact that other people may not know about a patient's adherence because they cannot monitor the patient 24 hours a day. Objective measures, which produce quantitative data, are often better, but they may also have flaws. For instance, quantity accounting or pill counting is sometimes used and ingenious devices have been created, such as Chung and Naya's (2000) track-cap. However, just because a pill has left a bottle, it doesn't mean that it has been taken. Another objective measure is to record the number of repeat prescriptions, assuming that if this is done, the patient must have taken the medicine. Perhaps the best way to record whether medicine has been taken is to take some physiological measure. For example, urine or blood tests could be used, or in one case, Lustman et al. (2000) recorded the blood sugar levels of people with diabetes. Simply, if the medicine has been taken then it will be recorded. Although such measures are reliable, it is unlikely that in everyday life anyone would regularly record a physiological state just to determine whether or not a person has taken their medicine.

Improving adherence

There are many ways in which adherence can be improved. Studies by Ley (1988) focused on what a medical practitioner could do to improve patients' adherence, such as emphasising key information, repeating instructions and not using medical jargon. A second strategy would be to provide patients with information, based on the assumption that patients are more likely to adhere if they have information and instructions to follow. This was shown in the heart health study by Lewin et al. (1992). A third approach is to use behavioural strategies. These can include tailoring treatments, sending prompts and reminders, or inventing novel ways of administering a medication.

For instance, Watt (2003) invented an ingenious device — the *funhaler* — to improve his son's use of an asthma inhaler. It teaches children how to inhale their asthma medication properly and at the same time makes it fun. The fun is created by use of breath-driven spinning toys and whistles. The stronger the child breathes the faster the toys spin and the louder the sound of the whistles. The behavioural aspect is that the more effectively a child inhales the medication the greater the reward enjoyed.

Health psychology: stress

This section looks at three aspects of stress: its causes, methods for measuring stress and techniques for managing it.

Causes of stress

There are many causes of stress. Stress may be due to life events, as suggested by Holmes and Rahe (1967), or stress may stem from everyday hassles, as suggested by Kanner et al. (1981). It may be that if we are a type A personality we will suffer more stress than if we are a type B personality, according to Friedman and Rosenman (1974). Another possible cause of stress is work.

Work stress

There may be a number of causes for work stress, including **task-related factors**, such as information overload, information under-load, and the pace of a machine. It may be caused by **interpersonal factors** such as role ambiguity or role conflict. Work stress may be due to **environmental factors** such as levels of noise, heat, lighting and similar factors.

A study by Johansson et al. (1978) looked at work stress in a Swedish sawmill where 'finishers' (workers who finish off the wood at the last stage of processing timber) were compared with a group of cleaners. The finishers' work was machine-paced and repetitive, and the finishers were isolated from other workers. In contrast, the cleaners' work was more varied, self-paced and allowed more time to socialise with other workers. Levels of stress were measured in two main ways: absenteeism through stress-related illness and levels of stress-related hormones recorded by analysis of urine sample. Compared to the cleaners, the finishers' level of absenteeism was much higher and they excreted far more stress hormones.

Hassles and life events

In 1967 Holmes and Rahe devised the **social readjustment rating scale** (SRRS) in order to examine the events and experiences in our lives that cause stress. They compiled a list of major and minor events and gave each a **rank** and a **mean value**. At the top of the list (rank 1 with a mean value of 100) was 'death of spouse'; at the bottom of the list (rank 43 and a mean value of 11) was 'minor violations of the law'. They believed that both positive as well as negative events cause stress, if these events were a change from normal routine. They thus listed Christmas as stressful, with 12 points and vacation/holiday with 13 points. A person's total SRRS is calculated by adding the mean value of any event that has happened in the previous 12 months. Holmes and Rahe found that people scoring 300 life change units or more were more susceptible to both physical and mental illness, ranging from sudden cardiac death to athletics injuries. There are numerous criticisms of the Holmes and Rahe SRRS, including the view that it is aimed at middle-aged men from the USA. There are various alternatives, such as that by Coddington (1972), produced for children and young adults.

While life events can cause stress, many only happen once in a lifetime. An alternative view is that stress is caused by the small everyday frustrations, such as the filling falling out of your sandwich, or the school bus being late. Kanner et al. (1981) called such events **daily hassles**. In the original study 100 adults completed the hassle scale once a month for 10 months and it was found that 'concerns about weight' and 'too many things to do' were at the top of the hassles list. The modified **hassles scale** now has 117 items. At the same time, the **uplifts scale** was devised and this includes 135 events that bring peace, satisfaction or joy, such as 'completing a task' and 'relating well to your lover'.

Lack of control

Studies show that people often experience stress when they believe they have little or no control over a situation. In the Johansson et al. study the sawmill finishers had little control over their work task so they experienced stress. Studies exploring the relationship between control, or lack of it, and stress have been conducted in the laboratory. For instance, Geer and Maisel (1972) showed two groups slides of aversive photographs of dead bodies. Data was gathered through galvanic skin response, measuring levels of autonomic arousal. The group with control were told they could stop the slide show by pressing a button. The group with no control were told nothing. The results revealed that the group without control found viewing the picture more stressful than the group with control.

Methods of measuring stress

A stressful event causes a response in both the sympathetic nervous system and the hormonal system. Two main types of hormones are secreted: catecholamines (such as adrenaline) and corticosteroids (such as aldosterone). The effect of adrenaline is to increase breathing, which increases the uptake of oxygen causing an increase in blood pressure and heart rate. Ultimately, there is an increase in muscle tension as the oxygenated blood feeds muscles, which are prepared for 'fight or flight'. Many recording devices can be used to assess this increased state of arousal. Additionally, people are aware of the stress psychologically and this too can be measured, mainly in the form of a questionnaire.

Physiological measures

Stress can be measured physiologically by any recording device that measures levels of arousal. Adrenaline causes an increase in blood pressure, which can be measured using a sphygmomanometer. Blood pressure is the first thing a doctor would check if a person reported feeling stressed. Goldstein et al. (1992) found that paramedics' blood pressure was higher during ambulance runs or when at the hospital, compared to other work situations or when at home. Galvanic skin response (GSR), which can also be used to measure stress (see Geer and Maisel's study above), calculates the electrical resistance of the skin, an indicator of the level of arousal in the autonomic nervous system. Although this measure would not be used to measure stress in real life, it can be used to monitor increased levels of arousal in laboratory studies.

Another way of measuring stress is through sample tests of either blood or urine, because any hormone will be present in the blood or secreted in urine. One study that recorded stress levels through sample testing was that of Lundberg in 1976 on train commuters in Sweden. It was found those riding for a shorter, but far more crowded, trip had much higher levels of stress hormone in their urine than those having a longer but less crowded ride.

Although all these measures are reliable, their validity is questionable because things other than stress can cause high blood pressure, autonomic arousal or the secretion of stress hormones.

Self-report measures

The psychological component of stress is usually measured by questionnaire. There are various stress questionnaires and each is linked to the perceived cause of stress. As mentioned above, Holmes and Rahe (1967) devised the SRRS to measure life events and Kanner et al. (1981) devised the hassles and uplifts scale to record daily hassles. In addition, Friedman and Rosenman (1974), also mentioned above, devised the 'type A personality questionnaire' to determine whether people have a type A or type B personality.

Combined approach

Stress has both a **physiological** component and a **cognitive** (or psychological) component. Each of these aspects can be measured. The physiological component can be measured using blood pressure tests, with GSR or by sample tests of blood or urine. However, although such measures are reliable, they are not valid — high blood pressure is not necessarily caused by stress (it might be due to narrowed arteries for example).

Alternatively, the cognitive or psychological component of stress can be measured using self-report questionnaires (e.g. life events, daily hassles, and type A personality). Although such questionnaires do measure what they claim to, people may respond to demand characteristics, give socially desirable answers, or bias the answers as they wish.

Stress can also be measured in other ways. For example, in the Johansson et al. (1978) study of work stress, levels of stress-related hormones were recorded by analysis of urine samples. In addition to this, levels of stress were measured through absenteeism caused by stress-related illness, showing that a combined approach is more useful than an individual measure.

Techniques for managing stress

There are a number of different ways in which stress can be managed. Those adhering to the medical approach would opt for **drug treatment**. Two common drugs are benzodiazepines and beta-blockers, which both reduce physiological arousal and feelings of anxiety. In addition to a medical approach, there are various psychological approaches, including cognitive and behavioural techniques. Some techniques for reducing stress are entirely **behavioural**, such as progressive muscle relaxation, and some techniques are entirely **cognitive**, such as imagery, or re-definition.

Cognitive

There are two stress-related techniques linked to Meichenbaum, both of which are abbreviated to SIT. One of these is **self-instructional training** and the other is **stress inoculation training**. Central to both is the cognitive component of stress, and in effect one is an extension of the other.

Self-instructional training (Meichenbaum 1977) focuses on the cognitive aspect of stress by getting a person to think of the maladaptive nature of his or her self-statements. Replacing maladaptive statements with positive, coping statements and relaxation leads the person to respond to stress in more positive ways.

Self-instructional training was the second component of Meichenbaum's (1988) wider **stress inoculation training**. This is based on the assumption that people experience stress because of the way they negatively interpret an event or situation. Thus by redefining a situation with positive thinking they are less likely to experience stress.

The process of inoculation has three stages:

(1) Conceptualisation: the trainer talks to the person about their stress experiences such as how they would normally cope with stress. Negative thought patterns are identified.

(2) Skill acquisition: this is where the person is educated about the physiological and cognitive aspects of stress. They also learn about the techniques used to manage stress including both behavioural and cognitive skills. Most important is the replacement of negative thought patterns with positive ones.

(3) Application and follow-through: the person then applies these new skills under supervision through a series of progressively more threatening situations to prepare them for real-life situations.

Behavioural

An effective way to manage stress is to apply the behavioural technique of biofeedback. This is the control of physiological functions through cognitive processing. For example, if we become aware that our heartbeat is too fast, we can slow it down just by thinking about it. A classic study in the use of biofeedback is that by Budzynski et al. (1970). Patients were suffering from chronic muscle contraction headaches caused by muscle tension in their foreheads. Budzynski et al. combined biofeedback with training in deep muscle relaxation in the experimental group of patients, and this group was compared with a control group of patients who received no biofeedback. The experimental group reported having fewer headaches than the control group. Furthermore, the benefits of the biofeedback were still effective after 3 months.

Social

In its simplest form, social support can enhance health and wellbeing. The benefits of social support are evident during periods of high stress but are relatively irrelevant during periods of low stress.

Social support has four main functions:

(1) Emotional support in the form of empathy, love and trust.

(2) Instrumental support such as financial support.

(3) Information support from those concerned in providing additional information.

(4) Appraisal support — feedback from people who are close and who are more likely to understand.

Social support can be provided for many reasons, and one study investigating the role of social support was that by Waxler-Morrison et al. (1991), who looked at the social support networks of 133 women with breast cancer. The study began after initial diagnosis with an assessment of social relationships and whether such networks increased the chances of survival 4 years later. Data were obtained through questionnaires and from hospital charts.

The findings showed that there is a better rate of survival in women with higher levels of social support, and significant features included:

- number of supportive friends
- number of other supportive persons
- whether the woman worked
- whether she was unmarried
- the extent of contact with friends
- the size of her social network

However, it was noted that although the social network is important, in this study the main factor influencing survival was the state of the cancer at the time of diagnosis.

Clinical psychology: dysfunctional behaviour and disorders

The OCR specification makes a distinction between **dysfunctional behaviours** and **disorders**, but these sections can be reorganised for clarity. Whereas *Diagnosing dysfunctional behaviours* and *Characteristics of disorders* are discrete categories, explanations and treatments of both dysfunctional behaviours and disorders are linked.

The *Explanations of dysfunctional behaviour* sub-section introduces the biological, behavioural and cognitive explanations in general terms whereas in the *explanations of one disorder* sub-section the general explanations are applied specifically to disorders. Similarly, the *Treatments for dysfunctional behaviour* sub-section introduces the biological, behavioural and cognitive treatments in general terms and in the *Treatments for one disorder* sub-section the general explanations are applied specifically to disorders.

Definitions of dysfunctional behaviour and disorders

Dysfunctional behaviour is an alternative label for atypical behaviour, which is an alternative label for abnormal behaviour. There are many different definitions of abnormal behaviour, and those most commonly cited in psychological literature include:
- **Deviation from statistical norms**. This is simply deviating from the norm or average as in a normal distribution curve. Anyone at either end of the curve is 'abnormal' or atypical and includes, for example, people who are either very tall

or very short, or people with a very low or a very high IQ. Members of MENSA would much prefer to be atypical rather than abnormal, hence the preferred use of the term atypical. But, members of MENSA may not be dysfunctional, highlighting the problematic nature of this term.

- **Deviation from social norms**. This refers to the commonly held norms of a society, which has expectations of how people should think and how they should behave. Such norms vary from one culture to another and they also change over time.
- **Deviation from ideal mental health**. If the characteristics of ideal mental health could be determined, then anyone not possessing those characteristics, or deviating from them, by definition would be abnormal. Although Jahoda (1958) has listed the features of good mental health there are still many problems with this definition.
- **Failure to function adequately**. This definition suggests that people who experience personal distress or discomfort will seek the help of a health care professional. By doing this they are adopting the 'sick role' and all that goes with it. However, such distress or discomfort may be a perfectly normal response to certain situations.
- **The elements of abnormality**. According to Rosenhan and Seligman (1989) there are seven elements of abnormality, and the more of the elements a person has, the greater the certainty that the person or behaviour is abnormal. The elements are:
  - suffering
  - maladaptiveness
  - irrationality and incomprehensibility
  - unpredictability and loss of control
  - vividness and unconventionality
  - observer discomfort
  - violation of moral and ideal standards

Categorising dysfunctional behaviour and disorders

In 1896 Kraepelin created the first comprehensive system of classification of psychological disorders, but this is not the only system.

The World Health Organization adopted a single system called the **International Classification of Diseases** and Related Health Problems (**ICD**). The ICD, now at version 10, listed *all* diseases, so a classification system for psychological problems only was devised in 1952 in the USA — the **Diagnostic and Statistical Manual** of Mental Disorders (or **DSM**), which is now in version IV (revised).

DSM has 16 categories of mental disorder whereas the ICD has 11. In terms of the OCR specification, only the following categories are pertinent:

- schizophrenia and related psychotic disorders
- mood (affective) disorders
- neurotic (anxiety) disorders

Each of these categories can be looked at a little more closely when considering characteristics of disorders. But why is a classification system needed?

- It provides a common set of terms so all can agree on meanings, allowing effective communication between professionals.
- It allows the understanding of the origin of disorders.
- It allows common treatment plans, resulting from effective diagnosis of a disorder.

Characteristics of disorders

Although DSM and ICD have broad categories, the OCR specification looks at specific examples and in this section the characteristics of the three named disorders are described:

- an **anxiety** disorder, such as a phobia
- a **psychotic** disorder, such as schizophrenia
- an **affective** disorder, such as bipolar disorder (manic depression)

An anxiety disorder

An anxiety disorder involves a general feeling of dread or apprehensiveness accompanied by various physiological reactions such as increased heart rate, sweating, muscle tension and rapid and shallow breathing.

DSM-IV(R) and ICD-10 label these disorders as **neurotic disorders**, such as:

- generalised anxiety disorder (free-floating anxiety), phobias, obsessive and compulsive disorders
- dissociative disorders, including amnesia, fugue and dissociative identity disorder (DID)
- somatoform disorders, including body dysmorphic disorder (BDD) and hypochondriasis.
- post-traumatic stress disorder (PTSD)

What are the typical features of a phobic?

People with a phobia only have problems when they come into contact with the object or situation causing their phobia, and most people will avoid such objects and situations in which they are present. On encountering the object or situation the response will be as described above and often it will be severe. But, for some people, such as agoraphobics, who may have not have left their home for 6 months or more, they will have closed curtains and never go to a door because of their fear of the outside world.

A psychotic disorder

Schizophrenia comes from the Greek terms *skhizein* (split) and *phren* (mind). There are five main types:

(1) **Disorganised (hebephrenic)** involves incoherence, disorganised behaviour, disorganised delusions and vivid hallucinations.

(2) **Simple** involves gradual withdrawal from reality.

(3) **Catatonic**, where there is impairment of motor activity, the person often holding the same position for hours or days.

(4) **Paranoid**, where the person has well-organised, delusional thoughts (and hallucinations), but a high level of awareness.

(5) **Undifferentiated/untypical**, which is a category for those who do not fit into any of the above categories.

DSM-IV(R) and ICD-10 label these disorders as **psychotic disorders and schizophrenia**, which include:

• schizophrenia (all types)
• delusional disorder, or paranoia
• various schizophreniform and schizoaffective disorders

What are the typical features of a schizophrenic?

Depending on the type of schizophrenia, the person may hear voices, which seem very real and are often abusive. They may have various kinds of hallucinations, smelling and hearing as well as seeing. There may be difficulty with thinking and concentration.

An affective disorder

The term 'affect' relates to mood or feelings. A person with depression will have intense feelings of depression or despair, while a person who is manic will have intense feelings of happiness and 'over-activity'. A person with bipolar disorder will have severe mood swings.

DSM-IV(R) and ICD-10 label such disorders as **mood (affective) disorders**, which include:

• depressive disorder, manic disorder and bipolar (manic-depressive)
• seasonal affective disorder
• post-natal depression and pre-menstrual disorder

What are the typical features of a person with bipolar disorder?

For depressive episodes:

• feelings of unhappiness, loss of interest, feeling inadequate and possibly thoughts of suicide
• continual urges to cry
• difficulty in concentrating and an inability to think positively, often with hopeless feelings of guilt
• difficulty in sleeping; possible loss of appetite and weight; avoiding other people.

For manic episodes:
- feeling very excited
- having lots of energy and enthusiasm, and quickly moving from one thing to another
- outbursts of exuberance, heightened good humour and often entertaining for those present
- talking quickly, feeling less inhibited and making spur-of-the-moment decisions

Biases in diagnosing dysfunctional behaviour and disorders

Classification systems have advantages, but there are problems and biases in classification systems and the diagnosis of disorders.

Reliability

This concerns the consistency of diagnosis. We would expect the same set of symptoms to be diagnosed in exactly the same way by any psychiatrist. One way to test this is to use inter-rater reliability, and many studies have compared the consistency of diagnoses. In one study Pedersen et al. (2001) found 71% of psychiatrists agreed with the ICD-10 definition of depression when assessing 116 patients.

Validity

Diagnosis may be consistent, but what if it is wrong? The classic study here is the AS core study by Rosenhan (1973). In nearly all cases the pseudo-patients were incorrectly diagnosed as having schizophrenia (at one point the symptom of hearing voices was diagnosed as manic depression). This means that the psychiatrists were reliable, but their diagnosis was not valid as the pseudo-patients were fake. However, the psychiatrists all made type 2 errors, which is a bias in diagnosis.

Type 1 and type 2 errors

It is hoped that any diagnosis should be correct, but it isn't always. It may be that a medical practitioner is in doubt about whether a person has an illness, whether physical or medical. If in doubt, it is safer for the practitioner to assume the person has an illness or disorder and request further tests or to observe for longer. To do this may be incorrect, and this is a type 2 error, but it is a safe decision. This is what happened to the psychiatrists in the Rosenhan case. However, to assume that a person is not ill, when in fact they are, amounts to negligence, and this type 1 error should be avoided by all medical practitioners.

Ethnocentrism

Littlewood (1992) questions the 'international' validity of DSM-IV(R) over the assumptions it makes about nuclear family life. Littlewood and Lipsedge (1989) looked at the very high incidence of schizophrenics in the UK from the Caribbean. It was discovered that only 15% had typical symptoms, the others had 'west Indian psychoses', a logical response to disadvantage and racism.

Gender bias

Ford and Widiger (1989) raise a fundamental question. Why are those involved in diagnosing and classifying disorders predominantly men, when those being diagnosed and treated are mainly women? Their main fear was that normal stereotypical gender roles might be incorrectly labelled as pathological. When presented with identical case histories, except for gender, 354 psychologists diagnosed women mainly with histrionic personality disorder, whereas men were more likely to be diagnosed with anti-social personality disorder.

Explanations of dysfunctional behaviours and disorders

Biological explanations

The biomedical model of health focuses only on biological factors to understand a person's illness and excludes psychological and social factors. The model includes all possible biological bases for behaviour — chemical, genetic, physiological, neurological and anatomical. The approach is summarised in a classic quotation from Maher (1966): 'Deviant behaviour is referred to as *psychopathology*, is classified on the basis of *symptoms*, the classification being called *diagnosis*, the methods used to try to change the behaviours are called *therapies*, and these are often carried out in *mental* or *psychiatric hospitals*. If the deviant behaviour ceases, the patient is described as *cured*.'

Assumptions of the biological approach

- The biological approach or biomedical model is based on the assumption that dysfunctional behaviour has a biological cause.
- Mental disorders are the same as physical illnesses but are just located in a different part of the body.
- Mental illnesses can be diagnosed and treated in the same ways as physical illnesses: mainly with drugs, but with the options of surgery or electro-convulsive therapy.

Genetic inheritance is an important cause of human behaviour including dysfunctional behaviour or disorders. Studies of identical (monozygotic) twins have revealed a high concordance rate for a number of conditions. If one twin has a disorder the likelihood that the other will also get it can be as high as 50%. Fraternal (dizygotic) twins also have a concordance rate, but it is much less than that for identical twins. Genes also determine levels of hormones and other biochemicals that influence behaviour.

Psychotic disorders

Statistics reveal that 1 in 10 people with schizophrenia have a parent with the illness. Gottesman and Shields (1972) examined the records of 57 schizophrenics between 1948 and 1964. In their sample 40% of the twins were monozygotic and 60% were dizygotic. They found concordance rates (the probability of a twin having schizophrenia if the other twin has it) of 42% for monozygotic twins and 9% for dizygotic twins. This provided evidence of a genetic link for schizophrenia.

Affective disorders

Depression also runs in families, and the closer the genetic relationship, the more likely people are to be diagnosed with the disorder. First-degree relatives (close family members, such as brothers, sisters, sons, daughters, fathers and mothers) share 50% of their genes. According to Oruc et al. (1998) first-degree relatives of people diagnosed with depression are two or three times more likely to be diagnosed with depression than those who are not first-degree relatives.

Anxiety disorders

There is some evidence for a genetic explanation for specific phobias. For example, Ost (1992) found those with a specific phobia for blood injuries had 60% of first-degree relatives who also had the same phobia.

For any genetic explanation it is important to realise that people do not inherit a specific gene for an illness, such as schizophrenia or depression. Rather, people inherit the vulnerability to it.

Behaviourist explanations

Classical conditioning was originally demonstrated by Pavlov in his experiments with dogs, and operant conditioning, based on reinforcement, was originally demonstrated by Skinner. Although there are many differences between these two behaviourist explanations, both make the assumption that dysfunctional behaviours are learned.

Assumptions of the behaviourist approach

- All behaviour is learned through the principles of classical conditioning (association) and operant conditioning (reinforcement).

- Dysfunctional (maladaptive) behaviour is learned in exactly the same way.
- Dysfunctional behaviour can be treated with behaviour therapies, or with behaviour modification, in which maladaptive behaviours are replaced with adaptive behaviours.

Anxiety disorder

The earliest example is the study by Watson and Raynor (1920), who **classically conditioned** little Albert. Initially, Albert was not afraid of animals, and his favourite was a white rat. But then, every time the rat was presented to Albert, a loud noise, made by banging two mental bars together, made him jump and frightened him. Albert associated the fear with the rat, and this fear of the rat generalised to other animals too. This demonstrated that fears and phobias can be learned.

Affective disorder

Lewinsohn (1974) believes that depression is caused by a **lack of positive reinforcement**. For example, if a person loses a job, there may be fewer opportunities for constructive behaviour and associated reward. Further, the person may engage in less social activity and the positive features of his/her life decrease even more. This low rate of positive reinforcement can lead the person into a negative spiral towards depression. In support of this theory Lewinsohn et al. (1979) found that the amount of positive reinforcement people receive in life is related to the presence or absence of depression. It was found that depressed participants reported fewer rewards than non-depressed subjects, and further that when there was an increase in the amount of positive reinforcement, their mood improved.

Cognitive explanations

The cognitive model focuses on the thoughts and interpretations that people have about their life, their abilities and their future. People sometimes have faulty logic and they think negatively and this leads them to behave in dysfunctional ways.

Assumptions of the cognitive approach

- Cognitive psychologists believe that thinking determines all behaviour and that dysfunctional behaviour is caused by inappropriate or faulty thought processes.
- Cognitive therapy involves helping people to restructure their thoughts, helping them to think more positively about themselves, their life and their future.

Affective disorder

Beck (1979) believes that people react differently to aversive stimuli because of the thought patterns that they have built up throughout their lives. Beck believes that **schemas** (core beliefs) are formed in early life. For example, if a person has developed a negative set of schemas, they may include a *self-blame schema* that makes the person feel responsible for all the things in their life that go wrong or an *inept-ness schema* that causes them to expect failure every time. These schemas and assumptions predispose the person to having negative automatic thoughts (NATs) but they will only surface if an event triggers them. When that happens, they are supported by **cognitive errors**, characteristic errors in the process of thinking that help to maintain the negative beliefs. Beck believes that depression results from the **negative cognitive triad**, comprising unrealistically negative views about (i) the *self*, (ii) the *world* and (iii) the *future*. Typical comments would include 'I'm totally useless' and 'I can't see a future any more'.

In his original experiments, Seligman discovered that dogs became helpless and depressed. However, this was not found in all cases. In later research he found that the original theory of **learned helplessness** failed to account for people's varying reactions to situations: sometimes learned helplessness remained specific to one situation but at other times it generalised across situations. Seligman (1979) suggested that a person's **attributional style** was the key to understanding why people responded differently to adverse events.

If a person makes an internal attribution (they are the cause) and if they believe that this is stable and global (the cause is consistent and this applies everywhere) then they may feel helpless and may experience depression. However, if they make other attributions (e.g. that the cause is external or situational; or unstable rather than stable, and specific rather than global), then helplessness and depression are unlikely to occur. Attributional style is assessed using the **attributional style questionnaire** (ASQ) and Seligman and others have found depression is associated with an internal/global/stable pattern. After therapy depression is again assessed and the attributional style is indeed less internal/global/stable (Seligman et al. 1988).

Anxiety disorder

Beck explains anxiety through a person possessing a different set of schemas to those that determine depression, which are also subject to the faulty negative logic of the cognitive biases.

DiNardo et al. (1988) go further than a behavioural explanation for anxiety. In their study it was found that only half of all people who had a traumatic experience with a dog, even when pain was inflicted, went on to develop a phobia of dogs. They also found that a comparable group of people who did not have a phobia of dogs reported that they had experienced a traumatic experience with a dog. This would contradict a behavioural explanation. DiNardo et al. (1988) believe that people who have a traumatic experience (e.g. with dogs) but do not develop a phobia must *interpret* the event differently from those who develop a phobia. They suggest it is an **exaggerated expectation of harm** that is the crucial factor in the development of a phobia, and that all those who had a phobia of dogs believed that fear and harm were the likely consequences of a negative encounter with a dog.

Psychodynamic explanations

The OCR specification does not mention the psychodynamic approach in relation to health and clinical psychology, but:

(1) the psychodynamic approach is a major contributor in both the explanation and treatment of dysfunctional behaviours and disorders and

(2) the psychodynamic approach does appear on the OCR specification as a perspective that you must cover, so it may appear on the synoptic paper G544

Freud believed that personality is made up of three subconscious structures: the **id**, the **ego** and the **superego**. When these three are balanced, a person is mentally stable and has no dysfunctional behaviour. Such balancing occurs as a child develops and passes through the five **psychosexual stages**. However, if there is an unresolved conflict in any of these stages then disorders, such as hysteria, result.

Assumptions of the psychodynamic approach

- Freud believed that the cause of dysfunctional behaviour was in the unconscious mind and related to unresolved conflicts of the id, ego and superego.
- The quality of early childhood experience is essential, especially those experiences in the first three psychosexual stages; otherwise, conflicts arise that cause later mental disorders.

Psychotic disorder

The psychodynamic approach views schizophrenia as the result of the disintegration of the ego. One function of the ego is to keep control of the id's impulses and a cold, rejecting mother can weaken the ego, which can mean that people lose contact with reality as they can no longer distinguish between themselves and others, their desires and fantasies, and reality.

Anxiety disorder

Conflict between the id and the ego causes anxiety. The id is the source of selfish urges, which can cause anguish, embarrassment and stress to a person, so they are repressed by the ego into the unconscious mind by defence mechanisms. One defence mechanism is displacement, meaning that anxiety may be displaced onto something else. The classic case study is that of Little Hans, who had a phobia of horses that was displaced from a fear of his father.

Treatments for dysfunctional behaviours and disorders

Biological treatments

The assumption here is that mental illnesses can be treated in the same ways as physical illnesses — mainly with drugs, but also with surgery and electro-convulsive therapy.

Affective disorder

In 1965 Schildkraut published *The Catecholamine Hypothesis of Affective Disorders*, in which where the chemical imbalance hypothesis for mental health disorders, especially for depression, was outlined. There are four main types of drug that relieve the symptoms of depression:

- tricyclics
- MAOIs (monoamine oxidase inhibitors)
- SSRIs (selective serotonin reuptake inhibitors)
- SNRIs (serotonin and noradrenaline reuptake inhibitors)

Generally, anti-depressants work by affecting neurotransmitters, and the chemicals most involved in depression are thought to be serotonin and noradrenaline, so SRRIs inhibit serotonin. Anti-depressants do not remove the *cause* of depression but instead relieve the symptoms.

Psychotic disorder

The first **antipsychotics** (or neuroleptics) were produced in the 1950s and the first such drug was chlorpromazine, which has a powerful calming effect and was known as the 'chemical lobotomy'. Other phenothiazines act as tranquillisers, sedating the patient and relieving the symptoms of psychosis such as delusions and hallucinations

The second generation of drug treatments were the **atypical anti-psychotics**, which act mainly by blocking dopamine receptors. They also reduce many of the side effects of the first-generation drugs. The third generation of drugs, such as Aripiprazole, are thought to reduce susceptibility to metabolic symptoms present in the second-generation atypical antipsychotics.

Electro-convulsive therapy (ECT) was originally developed as a treatment for schizophrenia in 1938 by Cerletti. In its early days it was given bilaterally, where electrodes are placed on each side of the patient's head. However, it was found to be ineffective in reducing psychotic symptoms. It is now used mainly as a treatment for severe depression and is usually only administered when drug treatment has failed. It is sometimes used to treat catatonic schizophrenia.

Psychosurgery has been used as a last resort when drugs and ECT have apparently failed. This involves either cutting out brain nerve fibres or ablating parts of the brain that are thought to be involved in the disorder. The most common form of psychosurgery is a pre-frontal lobotomy, usually used for schizophrenia. There are other types, including:

- **biomedial leucotomy**: for depression and obsessive-compulsive disorder
- **orbital leucotomy:** for depression, obsessive-compulsive disorder and extreme anxiety
- **bilateral leucotomy**: for severe depression
- **limbic leucotomy:** for abnormal aggression

Behavioural treatments

Therapies based on classical conditioning are often referred to as behaviour therapies, whereas those based on operant conditioning are known as behaviour modification.

Anxiety disorder

Systematic desensitisation is a therapy based on the principles of classical conditioning. It was developed by Wolpe in 1958, specifically for the counter-conditioning of fears, phobias and anxieties. The idea behind systematic desensitisation is to replace the conditioned fear, which is maladaptive, with one of relaxation, which is an adaptive and desirable response. The pairing of the feared stimulus with relaxation induces the desensitisation.

It involves three separate phases:

(1) The therapist and the person construct a **hierarchy of fearful situations**. This means coming up with a range of situations or events with which the fear is associated and arranging them in order from the least fearful to the most fearful.

(2) The person is trained in deep **muscle relaxation techniques**. This involves contracting and relaxing muscles throughout the body, gaining control of breathing and using visualisation techniques.

(3) The person is then brought into contact with the least fearful item in the hierarchy of the phobic stimulus, and the person uses the learned techniques to produce a state of relaxation. When relaxation has been achieved, the next item in the hierarchy is presented. This **continues systematically** until all the items in the hierarchy have been removed and the person is desensitised.

McGrath et al. (1990) found that systematic desensitisation was effective in 75% of people with specific phobias.

Psychotic disorder

A second behavioural treatment is based on positive reinforcement. Ayllon and Azrin (1968) outlined the **token economy system**, which involves giving tokens for good or desirable behaviour, which may be later exchanged for rewards. Such systems have worked well in schools and in open cast mines with regard to safety behaviour (e.g. Fox et al. 1987) and it has also been used for patients with schizophrenia. Paul and Lentz (1977) found that the use of tokens was successful in reducing bizarre motor behaviours and in improving social interactions with staff and other patients. However, the token economy system does not have any impact on hallucinations and delusions, and any improvements tend not to last once the patients are released.

Cognitive (and behavioural) treatments

Cognitive therapy aims to change the way a person thinks and so change the way the person feels or behaves.

Cognitive behaviour therapy (**CBT**) changes the way a person thinks (the cognitive part) *and* the way a person behaves (the behavioural part). It may focus on how a person responds to a particular situation. This is done not by going back to the *cause* of the problem, but by focusing on the **present symptoms**. It works by looking at how a person *thinks* about how an event has affected how he or she *felt* and what he or she *did*. If negative thoughts can be reinterpreted or changed for more positive or realistic **thoughts**, then the person will **feel** better and their **behaviour** will change.

Affective disorder

Beck et al. (1979) believe in **cognitive restructuring**. The aim is to restructure negative automatic thoughts (the biased information processing) with positive automatic thoughts. This done in a six-stage process, starting with an explanation of the therapy itself. Next the person is taught to identify unpleasant emotions, situations in which these occur and associated negative automatic thoughts. Then the person is taught to challenge the negative thoughts and replace them with positive thoughts. Finally the person can begin to challenge the underlying dysfunctional beliefs before the therapy ends.

The efficacy of cognitive therapy for depression has been demonstrated by Dobson (1989) in a meta-analysis of 28 clinical trials. He compared the scores on the Beck depression inventory (BDI) of those in cognitive therapy with patients in other therapies or undergoing no treatment. Using the BDI to record change between pre-treatment and post-treatment, on average the cognitive-therapy patients scored:

- 98% better than the control patients
- 70% better than those in anti-depressant drug treatments and
- 70% better than those in some other form of psychotherapy

Ellis (1962) outlined **rational emotive therapy**, which was developed into **rational emotive behaviour therapy** (**REBT**). Ellis focuses on how illogical beliefs are maintained through:

- A for the activating event, perhaps the behaviour or attitude of another person
- B for the belief held about A and
- C, which is the thoughts, feelings or behaviours resulting from A

Ellis describes the illogical or irrational beliefs using the terms **musterbating** (we *must* be perfect at all times) and **I-can't-stand-it-itis** (the belief that when something goes wrong it is a major disaster).

In order change to rational beliefs, Ellis expands the ABC model to include:

- D for disputing the irrational beliefs and
- E for the effects of successful disruption of the irrational beliefs

Anxiety disorder

Ost and Westling (1995) investigated the effectiveness of **cognitive behaviour therapy** (CBT) in the treatment of panic disorder. The outpatients in their sample were treated over 12 weekly sessions. The results revealed a significant reduction in the number of panic attacks in the patients, who were also panic-free at the follow-up. They also found that the treatment led to reductions in generalised anxiety, depression and cognitive misinterpretations.

Psychotic disorder

Sensky et al. (2000) have used CBT in the treatment of schizophrenia. The participants, from clinics in London and the north of England, had schizophrenia for at least 6 months, despite drug treatment with chlorpromazine. After 45-minute sessions for at least 2 months with CBT, patients showed significant improvements. At the 9-month follow-up evaluation, patients who had received CBT continued to improve and the results could not be attributed to changes in prescribed medication. It was concluded that CBT is effective in treating negative as well as positive symptoms in schizophrenia.

Approaches in psychology

Cognitive approach

Cognitive psychology is about mental processes such as remembering, perceiving, understanding and producing language, solving problems, thinking and reasoning. Sometimes people behave in logical ways and sometimes they behave irrationally. It is the task of cognitive psychologists to try to understand why people think as they do, and it is the task of health and clinical psychologists to try to understand such thought processes in health settings and as they apply to disorders and dysfunctional behaviours. For example, people may not take their medicine because of rational non-adherence: the person has thought about it and decided to stop taking the medicine. Another example is why people possess the illogical beliefs that can cause depression or anxiety.

Developmental approach

Developmental psychology is sometimes understandably, but misleadingly, thought of as child psychology, but a truly comprehensive developmental psychology should concern itself with the whole **lifespan** of human development. The developmental approach plays only a small part in health and clinical psychology. One contribution is in Freud's psychosexual stages, during which fixations and conflicts can lead to disorders such as phobias.

Physiological approach

Physiological psychology explores human behaviour and experience by looking at people as if they were biological machines. How much does our biology affect us and what other factors intervene to affect the response? Put another way, to what extent does our biology *determine* our behaviour? Physiology plays a major role in how we experience stress and earlier we looked at the role of hormones in the process. Physiological tests of blood and urine can determine whether or not people have taken their medicine and there are biological explanations for dysfunctional behaviours and disorders.

Social approach

Social psychology is concerned with the social side of human life. Social psychologists look at the numerous complex issues that surround human interaction and human relationships and how the *individual* behaves in various social contexts that both frame and direct their actions and experiences.

One of the A2 issues is how much importance should be given to the individual or to the situation in our explanations of social behaviour.

In health and clinical psychology patients interact with medical practitioners. This practitioner–patient relationship is crucial not only in determining satisfaction with the interaction but perhaps in determining whether or not people take their medicine. A further issue is the extent to which any dysfunctional behaviour or disorder is the result of the individual or the situation they are in. It may well be the effect of a combination of the two. For example, if an individual has an unpleasant experience with a dog, he/she may interpret the event in a particular way and become dog-phobic.

Psychology of individual differences

Psychology often makes *generalisations* about people, such as how people behave, think and feel. Although some of these general statements are useful, they ignore the *differences* between groups of people, and between individual people. Generalisations apply to most people for most of the time; they do not apply to everyone all of the time.

Individual differences are a major issue for health and clinical psychologists. Many explanations for dysfunctional behaviours and disorders assume that people are all the same (assuming further that all people can be treated in the same way) when they are not. The task for psychology is to identify the features that we *share* with other people yet still acknowledge the *differences* between individuals.

Perspectives in psychology

There are a number of perspectives in psychology. You are introduced to two at AS and others may appear at A2 depending on which options you choose. For example, the *Psychology and Education* option introduces humanistic theories of motivation. At AS the two perspectives are the behaviourist and the psychodynamic, followed through at A2 and assessed in Unit G544.

Psychodynamic perspective

The psychodynamic perspective does not appear in the OCR specification for health and clinical psychology despite its major contribution to this area. This perspective is considered in this guide because it can offer an alternative viewpoint on disorders and dysfunctional behaviours. Based on the work of Freud, it emphasises the role of the unconscious mind (the id, ego and superego) and the influence that childhood experiences have on our future lives.

A person is psychologically healthy when there is a balance between the id, ego and superego with these opposing forces under control. A psychologically unhealthy person is seen as having neuroses because of unresolved conflicts during the developmental stages in childhood.

Behaviourist perspective

The behaviourist perspective takes the view that the subject matter of psychology should have standardised procedures, with the emphasis on the study of observable behaviour that can be measured objectively and not on the mind or consciousness.

The work of Pavlov and Skinner features strongly in health and clinical psychology because, as shown in the work of Watson and little Albert, it explains how anxiety disorders are learned. The work of Wolpe on systematic desensitisation shows that people can be desensitised to phobias. More than this, combined with a cognitive approach, CBT is the modern treatment for most affective, psychotic and anxiety-based disorders.

Methods in psychology

The OCR specification lists four different methods: experimental (divided into laboratory and field), case study, self-report and observation.

Many studies carried out for health and clinical psychology involve patients with real problems. In some instances the patients are involved in trials of new drugs or other treatments and they are compared to a control group.

Experimental method

Description
- **Experiment:** a form of research in which variables are manipulated in order to discover cause and effect. It is commonly performed in a laboratory.
- **Field experiment:** a study that follows the logic of an experiment, but is conducted in the outside world rather than in the laboratory.
- **Natural experiment** (also called 'quasi-experiment'): an event in which variables change as a result of natural or other circumstances, such that the outcome of these changes can then be studied.

Examples
- **Laboratory:** Janis and Feshback; Leventhal et al.
- **Field:** Johansson et al.; Cowpe; McVey and Stapleton; Bulpitt
- **Natural:** many studies involving *patients*

Strengths of experimental method
- Manipulation of one variable and the control of confounding variables means that it is more likely to discover cause and effect.
- It is possible to control many confounding variables.
- The laboratory setting should ease the process of data collection e.g. use of one-way mirror or recording devices (such as sphygmomanometer).
- As the study is in a laboratory, participants must have given consent, which may make the study more ethical.

Weaknesses of experimental method
- Controlling variables is reductionist, as it is unlikely that any behaviour exists in isolation from other behaviours.
- The task performed is unlikely to be true to real life; the setting itself is low in ecological validity.
- The participants know they are taking part in a study and may respond to demand characteristics.

Case-studies method

Description
Case studies involve a detailed description of a particular individual or group under study or treatment.

Examples
Freud; Watson and Raynor

Strengths of case-studies method
- The data gathered are rich and detailed.
- Participants are often studied over a period of time and so developmental changes can be recorded. This is longitudinal and it often means that the data gathered are detailed.
- They are ecologically valid because the participant may be studied as part of his or her everyday life.
- Rare or unique behaviours can be studied in detail.
- The sample *may* be self-selecting, which means that the participants are not chosen by researchers.

Weaknesses of case-studies method
- There may be only one participant (or very few) involved, and so any conclusions cannot be generalised to other people.
- The participant may be unique, possibly 'not normal' in some way. This may mean that the researchers may not know how to proceed and they may draw false conclusions.
- The researchers may become emotionally attached to the participant if only one person is studied over a period of time.

Self-report method

Description
- Self-reports involve research that uses participants' own accounts of their behaviour or experience.
- Self-report methods include questionnaires, interviews, thinking aloud and diary methods.

Examples
Holmes and Rahe; Kanner et al.; Friedman and Rosenman; Seligman.

Strengths of self-report method
- The participants are given the opportunity to express their feeling and explain their behaviour.
- The quality and richness of the data gained often outweigh any weaknesses.
- The participants may be less likely to drop out of the study if they feel as though they are 'more than a number'.

Weaknesses of self-report method
- The data may be unique and not comparable with others.
- The participants may provide socially desirable responses/respond to demand characteristics.
- Just because the self-report data from a questionnaire is given a number it does not automatically make that data more scientific.

Observation method

Description

In an observation the researcher will simply observe behaviour and attempt to record the behaviour that he or she sees. Observations can be natural (of some real-life event and without those being observed being aware of it), or they can be controlled (which may or may not be in a laboratory and those being observed may not be aware of it). Behaviour can be observed by an observer acting as a participant (participant observation).

Examples

- Rosenhan

Strengths of observation method

- The observed behaviour is natural and can be objectively measured.
- The data are often quantitative, involving response categories.
- The participants may be unaware of the observation, and so are unaffected by demand characteristics.

Weaknesses of observation method

- The participants cannot explain why they behaved in particular way.
- The observer's view may be obstructed; observations may not be reliable.
- Observations in certain situations may not be replicable.

Issues in psychology

There are many issues to debate in psychology, and the OCR AS specification focuses on just four: **ethics**, **ecological validity**, **longitudinal and snapshot**, and **qualitative and quantitative** data. For A2, the OCR specification introduces a number of new issues, as described below.

Determinism and free will

Description

Determinism is the view that we have no or little control over our behaviour or our destiny, but are controlled by factors such as our biology or genetics, or by the reinforcements we are given. We can, therefore, have biological determinism and environmental determinism. The opposite is free will — the extent to which people have a genuine choice of behaviour. Possibilism and probabilism are intermediates between free will and determinism.

Examples

- To explain schizophrenia through genetics is biological determinism.
- To explain the learning of all phobias by association is determinist.

- Restructuring negative thoughts for positive ones to raise awareness in a person and allow them to realise that they do have a choice is an example of free will.

Strengths of determinism
- Determinism is the purpose and goal of science: to explain the causes of behaviour.
- Determinism is more acceptable to society with its explanations, scientific basis and objectivity.

Weaknesses of determinism
- Determinism can never fully explain behaviour; behaviour may be far too complex.
- Determinism is often reductionist.
- People think they have free will and this has implications for determinism.

Reductionism and holism

Description
Reductionism is the process of explaining complex psychological phenomena by reducing them to their component parts. This is opposite to holism — the view that the whole is greater than the sum of the parts.

Examples
- Genetic explanations for disorders are reductionist — e.g. Gottesman and Shields (1972); Ost (1992); Oruc et al. (1998).
- The assumption that medical illnesses are the same as physical illnesses.
- Seligman originally reducing depression to nothing more than learned helplessness, then reformulating it to include attributions.

Strengths of reductionism
- In theory it is easier to study one component rather than several interacting components.
- If one component is isolated and others are controlled then study is more objective/scientifically acceptable.

Weaknesses of reductionism
- Components may be difficult to isolate and so manipulate.
- If an isolated behaviour is studied in a laboratory it may lack ecological validity.
- Any behaviour may not be meaningful if studied in isolation from the wider social context.

Nature–nurture

Description
Nature in this sense refers to the part of us that is inherited and genetic, as distinct from nurture, which refers to all influences after birth (i.e. experience). The interactionist version of this debate considers what percentage is inherited and what is learned.

Examples
- The genetic view of schizophrenia, e.g. Ost (1992); or of depression, e.g. Oruc et al. (1998).
- The learning of phobias through classical conditioning, e.g. Watson and Raynor (1920)

Strengths of studying nature and nurture
- It can help us identify behaviours that are inherited and learned, or allow us to consider the relative contribution of each.
- To discover that some behaviours are due to nature and so are not due to inappropriate upbringing by parents.
- To answer one of the ongoing puzzles of life.

Weaknesses of studying nature and nurture
- It is simplistic to divide explanations into either nature or nurture; how much behaviour is a combination of each (and what percentage is it?)
- To discover that a particular capacity or behaviour is inherited, for example that intelligence is inherited, may lead some to assume many more behaviours are inherited and fail to take into account the effects of the environment.

Ethnocentrism

Description
The term comes from the word 'ethnos', meaning 'nation' in modern Greek and 'kentro' meaning 'centre'. Specifically, this means that we are 'nation-centred' but psychologists are often less global and take it to mean much smaller social groupings. Thus, it often refers to the belief that our own viewpoint, or the viewpoint of people like us, is superior to that of others, particularly people who are different in some way.

Examples
- Assuming that any health belief model or method of health promotion (e.g. Cowpe 1989) will be applicable anywhere in the world.
- Assuming that the Western view of work stress (e.g. Johansson et al. 1978) will apply in Eastern societies.
- Assuming that life events (Holmes and Rahe 1967), type A personalities (Friedman and Rosenman 1974) and daily hassles (Kanner et al. 1981) apply universally.
- Biases over the validity of DSM-IV(R) when applied to non-Western countries.

Strengths of studying ethnocentrism
- It allows us to discover that not all cultures are the same; to discover the diversity of behaviour and experience that people all over the world have.
- It may allow discovery of the causes of prejudice and discrimination; to realise that our values are not the only ones possible; it educates us not to make value judgements.
- It may allow us to discover what behaviours are inherited and what behaviours are learned, i.e. by conducting cross-cultural studies.

Weaknesses of studying ethnocentrism

- Many cultures have different philosophies; they are different (not inferior or superior) and cannot be compared. Some cultures are based on cooperation; others are based on conflict.
- Researchers may speak a different language from participants: there may be problems in the giving of instructions and the understanding of tasks; there may be misinterpretation of behaviour by experimenters.
- Behaviours change over time and some cultures may change more quickly than others. What is found at one point in time may change rapidly.
- The sample from any study may be very small, or not representative, or be from one culture and so cannot be generalised to all cultures. To do this would be ethnocentric.

Psychology as a science

Description

The experimental method is scientific and aims to manipulate one variable, control all extraneous variables and so establish a cause and effect relationship. Also scientific is the gathering of quantitative data to which statistics can be applied.

Examples

- Biological explanations and treatments of mental illnesses.
- Observable behaviour as in the case of little Albert (Watson and Raynor 1920).
- Physiological measures of stress (e.g. Geer and Maisel 1972).

Strengths of psychology as a science

- The manipulation of one variable and controls means that cause and effect are more likely. More control over many extraneous variables is possible.
- Science is more acceptable in society.
- A laboratory setting can facilitate data collection e.g. use of one-way mirror or recording devices.

Weaknesses of psychology as a science

- It may be reductionist. Does any behaviour exist in isolation from others?
- If subject matter is observable behaviour the underlying reasons for a behaviour may not be known.
- The subject matter of psychology is much more than that of traditional science.

Individual and situational explanations

Description

Individual and situational explanations refer to the way we describe the cause of a behaviour as being due to something in that person (individual or dispositional) or as a response to the situation that the person is in.

Examples

- The health belief model includes individual perceptions and situational modifying factors.

- An individual has negative thoughts that extend to all situations, e.g. Beck (1967).
- The work situation of the finishers in the Swedish sawmill (Johansson et al. 1978) caused their individual stress.

Strengths of studying individual and situational explanations
- If we can determine which behaviours are individual and which are situational, such findings may be useful for society.
- Discovering that behaviour may involve a complex interaction between the two opens up new directions for further study.

Weaknesses of studying individual and situational explanations
- It can be difficult to separate the effects of a situation from the disposition of a participant.
- How can situations be investigated? If investigated in a laboratory there is low ecological validity; if investigated in a natural setting the situation may be difficult to control.
- It may not be individual or situational as exclusives, but a complex interaction of the two.

Usefulness of psychological research

Description
This examines the contribution that psychology makes to human welfare. Miller (1969) argued that psychology should aim to improve people's quality of life, and that it should be useful to everyone. Not everything psychologists study and claim is useful, but they often make the world a more interesting place in which to live.

Examples
- The usefulness of many therapies such as cognitive behaviour therapy (CBT) (e.g. Sensky et al. 2000).
- The usefulness of the token economy system for schizophrenics (e.g. Paul and Lentz 1977).
- The usefulness of electroconvulsive therapy or psychosurgery.

Strengths of useful psychological research
- If research is useful, it can be of benefit to society. It can improve the world in which we live.
- If research is useful, it enhances the value of psychology as a subject

Weaknesses of studying usefulness of psychological research
- A study must be ethical — participants should give informed consent and not be deceived. But a study may need to be unethical to be truly useful.
- A study should be ecologically valid. Studies conducted in a laboratory may not be useful as they are low in ecological validity.
- A study should use a representative sample and be generalisable. Useful research should apply worldwide so there is no ethnocentrism.
- A study should be not be reductionist; it should not only apply in isolation from other behaviours but in various contexts.

References

Ayllon, T. and Azrin, N. H. (1968) *The Token Economy: A Motivational System, for Therapy and Rehabilitation,* Appleton Century Crofts.

American Psychiatric Association (1994) *Diagnostic and Statistical Manual of Mental Disorders (DSM–IV)* (4th edn), APA.

Bandura, A. (1977) 'Self-efficacy', *Psychological Review,* Vol. 84, pp. 191–215.

Beck, A. T. (1967) *Depression: Causes and Treatment*, University of Philadelphia Press.

Beck, A. T., Rush, A. J., Shaw, B. F. and Emery, G. (1979) *Cognitive Therapy for Depression*, Guilford, New York.

Becker, M. H. and Rosenstock, I. M. (1984) 'Compliance with medical advice', in A. Steptoe and A. Matthews (eds) *Health Care and Human Behaviour,* Academic Press.

Bridge, L. R., Benson, P., Pietroni, P. C. and Priest, R. G. (1988) 'Relaxation and imagery in the treatment of breast cancer', *British Medical Journal*, Vol. 297, pp. 1169–72.

Budzynski, T. H., Stoyva, J. and Adler, C. S. (1970) 'Feedback-induced muscle relaxation: Application to tension headache', *Journal of Behaviour Therapy and Experimental Psychiatry*, Vol. 1, pp. 205–11.

Bulpitt (1988) cited in R. M. Kaplan, T. L. Patterson and J. F. Sallis, *Health and Human Behavior*, McGraw-Hill.

Chung, K. F. and Naya, I. (2000) 'Compliance with an oral asthma medication: a pilot study using an electronic monitoring device', *Respiratory Medicine*, Vol. 94, pp. 852–58.

Cowpe, C. (1989) 'Chip pan fire prevention: 1976–1984', in C. Channon (ed.) *Twenty Advertising Case Histories* (2nd series), Cassell.

Dannenberg, A., Gielen, A. C., Beilenson, P. L., Wilson, M. H. and Joffe, A. (1993) 'Bicycle helmet laws and educational campaigns: an evaluation of strategies to increase children's helmet use', *American Journal of Public Health*, Vol. 83, No. 5.

Di Nardo, P. A., Guzy, L. T. and Bak, R. M. (1988) 'Anxiety response patterns and etiological factors in dog-fearful and non-fearful subjects', *Behaviour Research and Therapy,* Vol. 26, pp. 245–51.

Dobson, K. S. (1989) 'A meta-analysis of the efficacy of cognitive therapy for depression', *Journal of Consulting and Clinical Psychology*, Vol. 57, No. 3, pp. 414–19.

Ellis, A. (1962) *Reason and Emotion in Psychotherapy*, Life Stuart, New York.

Ellis, A. (1991) 'The revised ABC of rational emotive therapy', *Journal of Rational Emotive and Cognitive Behaviour Therapy*, Vol. 9, pp. 139–92.

Ford, M. R. and Widiger, T. A. (1989) 'Sex bias in the diagnosis of histrionic and anti-social personality disorders', *Journal of Consulting and Clinical Psychology*, Vol. 57, No. 2, pp. 301–05.

Fox, D. K., Hopkins, B. L. and Anger, W. K. (1987) 'The long-term effects of a token economy on safety performance in open-pit mining', *Journal of Applied Behaviour Analysis*, Vol. 20, Issue 3, pp. 215–24.

Friedman, M. and Rosenman, R. H. (1974) *Type A Behavior and Your Heart*, Knopf.

Freud, S. (1905) 'Analysis of a phobia of a five-year-old boy', *Pelican Freud Library*, Vol. 8.

Geer, J. and Maisel, E. (1972) 'Evaluating the effects of the prediction-control confound', *Journal of Personality and Social Psychology*, Vol. 23, No. 3, pp. 314–19.

Goldstein, I. B., Jamner, L. D. and Shapiro, D. (1992) 'Ambulatory blood pressure and heart rate in paramedics during a work day and a day off', *Health Psychology*, Vol. 11, pp. 48–54.

Gottesman, I. I. and Shields, J. (1972) *Schizophrenia and Genetics: A Twin Study Vantage Point*, Academic Press.

Holmes, T. H. and Rahe, R. H. (1967) 'The Social Readjustment Rating Scale', *Journal of Psychosomatic Research*, Vol. 11, No. 2, pp. 213–18.

Jahoda, M. (1958) *Current Concepts of Positive Mental Health*, Basic Books.

Janis, I. and Feshbach, S. (1953) 'Effects of fear-arousing communications', *Journal of Abnormal and Social Psychology*, Vol. 48, pp. 78–92.

Johansson, G., Aronsson, G. and Lindström, B. O. (1978) 'Social psychological and neuroendocrine stress reactions in highly mechanised work', *Ergonomics*, Vol. 21, Issue 8, August, pp. 583–99.

Kanner, A. D., Coyne, J. C., Schaefer, C. and Lazarus, R. S. (1981) 'Comparison of two modes of stress measurement: Daily hassles and uplifts versus major life events', *Journal of Behavioural Medicine*, Vol. 4, No. 1, pp. 1–39.

Leventhal, H., Watts, J. C. and Pagano, F. (1967) 'Effects of fear and instructions on how to cope with danger', *Journal of Personality and Social Psychology*, Vol. 6, No. 3, pp. 313–21.

Lewin, B., Robertson, I., Cay E. L., Irving J., Campbell, M. A. (1992) 'Effects of self-help post myocardial infarction rehabilitation on psychological adjustment and use of health services', *Lancet*, 339, pp. 1036–40.

Lewinsohn, P. M. (1974) 'A behavioural approach to depression' in R. Friedman and M. Katz (eds) *The Psychology of Depression: Contemporary Theory and Research*, Winston/Wiley.

Lewinsohn, P. M., Youngren, M. A. and Grosscup, S. J. (1979) 'Reinforcement and depression', in R. A. Depue (ed.) *The Psychobiology of Depressive Disorders*, Academic Press, pp. 291–316.

Ley, P. (1988) *Communicating with patients*, Croom Helm.

Littlewood, R. (1992) 'Psychiatric diagnosis and racial bias: empirical and interpretive approaches', *Social Science and Medicine*, No. 34, pp. 141–149.

Littlewood, R. and Lipsedge, M. (1989) *Aliens and Alienists: Ethnic Minorities and Psychiatry*, Unwin Hyman.

Lustman, P. J., Freedland, K. E., Griffith, L. S., Clouse, R. E. (2000) 'Fluoxetine for depression in diabetes: a randomized double-blind placebo-controlled trial', *Diabetes Care*, Vol. 23, No. 5, pp. 618–23.

Lundberg, U. (1976) 'Urban commuting: crowdedness and catecholamine excretion', *Journal of Human Stress*, Vol. 2, No. 3, pp. 26–32.

Maher, B. D. (1966) *Principles of Psychopathology: An Experimental Approach*, McGraw-Hill.

Meichenbaum, D. (1977) *Cognitive Behaviour Modification: An Integrative Approach*, Plenum.

Meichenbaum, D. and Deffenbacher J. L. (1988) 'Stress Inoculation Training', *The Counseling Psychologist*, Vol. 16, No. 1, pp. 69–90.

McGrath, P. A. (1990) *Pain in Children: Nature Assessment and Treatment*, Guildford Press.

McVey, D. and Stapleton, J. (2000) 'Can anti-smoking television advertising affect smoking behaviour? Controlled trial of the Health Education Authority for England's anti-smoking TV campaign. Tobacco Control 2000', *British Medical Journal*, 9, pp. 273–82.

Miller, G. A. (1969) 'Psychology as a means of promoting human welfare', *American Psychologist*, 24, pp. 1063–75.

Oruc, L., Ceric, I. and Loga, S. (1998) 'Genetic mood disorders — an overview part one', *Medicinshi Archiv*, Vol. 52, pp. 107–12.

Oruc, L., Ceric, I. and Loga, S. (1998) 'Genetic mood disorders — an overview part two', *Medicinshi Archiv*, Vol. 52, pp. 167–73.

Ost, L.-G. (1992) 'Blood and injection phobia: background and cognitive, physiological and behavioral variables', *Journal of Abnormal Psychology*, Vol. 101, pp. 68–74.

Ost, L.-G. and Westling, B. E. (1995) 'Applied relaxation vs cognitive behavior therapy in the treatment of panic disorder', *Behaviour Research and Therapy*, Vol. 33, No. 2, pp. 145–58.

Paul, G. L. and Lentz, R. J. (1977) *Psychosocial Treatment of Chronic Mental Patients: Milieu versus Social-learning Programs*, Harvard University Press.

Pedersen, S. H., Stage, K. B., Bertelsen, A., Grinsted, P., Kragh-Sorensen, P. and Sorensen, T. (2001) 'ICD-10 criteria for depression in general practice', *Journal of Affective Disorders*, Vol. 65, pp. 191–94.

Rosenhan, D. (1973) 'On being sane in insane places', *Science*, 197, pp. 250–58.

Rosenman, D. L. and Seligman, M. E. P. (1995) *Abnormal Psychology* (3rd edn), WW Norton and Co.

Rotter, J.B. (1966) 'Generalised expectancies for internal vs external control of reinforcement', *Psychological Monographs*, Vol. 80, No. 1, pp. 1–28.

Schildkraut, J. J. (1965) 'The catecholamine hypothesis of affective disorders: a review of supporting evidence', *American Journal of Psychiatry*, Vol. 122, pp. 509–22.

Seligman, M. E. P., Castellon, C., Cacciola, J., Schulman, P., Luborsky, L., Ollove, M. and Downing, R. (1988) 'Explanatory style change during cognitive therapy for unipolar depression', *Journal of Abnormal Psychology*, Vol. 97, No. 1, pp. 13–18.

Seligman, M. E. P., Abramson, L. Y., Semmel, A. and Von Beyer, C. (1979) 'Depressive attributional style', *Journal of Abnormal Psychology*, Vol. 88, pp. 242–47.

Sensky, T., Turkington, D., Kingdon, D., Scott, J. L., Scott, J., Siddle, R., O'Carroll, M. and Barnes, T. R. E. (2000) 'A randomized controlled trial of cognitive-behavioral therapy for persistent symptoms in schizophrenia resistant to medication', *Archives of General Psychiatry*, Vol. 57, pp. 165–72.

Thornton, J., Rossiter, J. and White, L. (2000) 'The persuasive effectiveness of varying levels of fear appeals: an anti-speeding advertising experiment', *Proceedings of the Australian and New Zealand Marketing Academy Conferences*, Griffith University, Queensland, Australia.

Wallston, K. A., Strudler-Wallston, B. and CeVellis, R. (1978) 'Development of the multidimensional health locus of control (MHLC) scales', *Health Education Monographs,* Vol. 6, pp. 161–70.

Wolpe, J. (1958) *Psychotherapy by Reciprocal Inhibition,* Stanford University Press.

Watson, J. B. and Raynor, R. (1920) 'Conditioned emotional responses', *Journal of Experimental Psychology*, Vol. 3, pp. 1–14.

Watt, P. M., Clements, B., Devadason, S. G. and Chaney, G. M. (2003) 'Funhaler spacer: improving adherence without compromising delivery', *Archives of Disease in Childhood*, Vol. 88, pp. 579–81.

Waxler-Morrison, N., Hislop, T. G., Mears, B. and Kan, L. (1991) 'Effects of social relationships on survival for women with breast cancer: a prospective study', *Social Science and Medicine*, Vol. 33, pp. 177–83.

Questions
&
Answers

The *Options in Applied Psychology* exam paper for Unit G543 lasts 1 hour 30 minutes and the format is as follows:

- Answer **two** questions from **one** option (health and clinical psychology) and **two** questions from another option (forensic **or** sport **or** education).
- For each chosen option there will be **four** questions and you can choose any **two** from the four available.

Examiner's comments

All candidate responses are followed by examiner's comments. These are preceded by the icon **e** and indicate where credit is due. In the weaker answers, they also point out areas for improvement, specific problems and common errors such as lack of clarity, weak or non-existent development, irrelevance, misinterpretation of the question and mistaken meanings of terms.

The mark schemes for OCR psychology are banded, so the task for the examiner is to decide which mark scheme band an answer should be in and then determine a specific mark.

Healthy living: health promotion

(a) Describe one technique used to promote health. (10 marks)

(b) Discuss the effectiveness of health promotion techniques. (15 marks)

This question is based on the *Healthy living* section of the specification, on the sub-section: *Methods of health promotion and supporting evidence*. Answers to the question could involve a media campaign, legislation or fear arousal. Question part (a) is AO1, knowledge and understanding.

Question part (b) must focus specifically on the effectiveness of the health promotion techniques (*plural*) and is AO2: application of knowledge and understanding.

■ ■ ■

Answer to question 1: candidate A

(a) 'Methods used by psychologists in health promotion' is a study carried out by Janis et al. that tried to promote dental hygiene and showed that producing images of gum disease was interesting and kept the person's attention but producing a lighter advert without pictures of actual problems was taken into consideration more as the study showed that people who saw the lighter images improved dental hygiene more than those who saw the harsh images. Another method used by health psychologists is that psychologists went to a coal pit workforce and provided them with a free check up of everything, for example heart rate. Then once the result had come through the workers had one to one consultation with the doctors going through factors such as heart disease and the workers were all given information on how to improve their health. A follow up test 6 months later shows that the workers had improved their health, for example they had increased the amount of exercise they did, increased their vegetable and fruit intake, wore their seatbelts more often etc. Another method used to promote health is to make people aware of all the problems concerned with the issue, for example smoking. It was found that if you tell teenagers not to smoke, they were likely to do it. Instead it was suggested that teenagers were told what to do, as in how to handle peer pressure.

This candidate goes straight to a description of a study without identifying the health-promotion technique. Although the technique is recognised as fear arousal by the examiner, the candidate does not seem to be aware of this. The study described is appropriate and this is the exemplar study stated in the specification. The candidate then goes on to describe in detail a second technique. At least, this time he/she does say that 'the workers were all given information' suggesting that this is an example of the 'providing information' technique. However, the details of the study are not made particularly clear. A third technique is suggested, but it is unclear what this technique is.

A major problem with this answer is that the question requires *one* technique and the candidate describes two, and possibly three. Only one technique can be credited, but as the knowledge and detail are similar in the first two techniques, it does not matter which one is marked and which is ignored. In relation to the mark scheme: terminology is basic; the description of evidence is generally accurate but it lacks detail. It is organised, but grammar is poor. (Note the lack of punctuation in the opening lines.) This answer would be at the bottom end of the 3–5 mark band.

(b) The effectiveness of trying to promote good heath with any area is that people may not feel as if they have a problem, or will not admit to it. This is the first stage of six when you realise you may be addicted. Another reason for lack of effectiveness could be that people have individual differences. Just because some people do not smoke is it fair to make smokers pay high prices for their cigarettes and have campaigns to try to help them stop smoking if they do not see anything wrong with it? Another difficulty in effectiveness of good health is the locus of control of different people. For example some people have an internal locus of control whereas some people have external control. Those with internal control may feel they have no control of their lives and that they know what they are doing whereas those with an external locus of control may feel that they need to give up doing what they do because of the promotions to help people quit. Everyone is different though and it is hard to generalise unless there is a large representative sample. Another issue that should be taken into account is ethics. Is it ethical to ask people about their poor habits? They may feel stressed if you give them lots of information about their bad habits and the consequences. A person should never feel in a worse state of mind after the experiment than they were before. Another problem that arises with trying to promote good health is, someone may have a different perspective of good health from what someone else does for example.

The candidate makes the assumption that effectiveness is whether a technique helps people to change their habits successfully, and the focus throughout is on the person, rather than the actual technique. It is as if the candidate is answering a slightly different question, such as 'What are the difficulties when trying to change people's poor lifestyles?' There are a number of evaluative points in the answer, but they are not focused and could be argued to be of peripheral relevance to the question. Each point is limited in its description and there are no supporting examples. The quality of grammar is poor. Overall, this answer would be in the bottom band, scoring no more than 3 marks out of the 15 available.

■ ■ ■

Answer to question 1: candidate B

(a) The technique I have chosen to write about is the fear arousal technique, rather than legislation or media campaigns that provide information. The aim of this technique is to scare a person to give up some unhealthy behaviour and instead begin a healthier lifestyle. Perhaps the first study to use fear arousal was the 1953 Janis and Feshback study on oral hygiene, but I have decided to concentrate on the much better 1967 Leventhal, Watts and Pagano study on smoking. They conducted a laboratory experiment on smokers who were asked to complete a questionnaire on their attitudes about smoking and their desire to quit. All partici- pants then watched a film of a smoking machine to show the harmful effects of it. They were also given some information about the bad effects of smoking. Then the smokers were divided into two groups. One group did nothing more because what they had seen so far made them the moderate-fear group. The high-fear group were then shown an additional film, which was of an operation of a cancerous lung being removed from a smoker. Apparently this was so bad that some participants had to leave the room. There was no control group and no low- fear group. After the presentations, the participants answered the same questions as they had answered prior to the experiment. The results showed that partici- pants in the high fear arousal condition said they would give up smoking. Leventhal concluded that the high fear arousal condition was more effective in changing people's attitudes and intentions regarding smoking. This contradicts the Janis and Feshback findings because they suggested a moderate fear level was best. However, the Leventhal study is less ethical than the Janis study. The Leventhal experiment was snapshot and not longitudinal, because participants were only involved for an hour or so. It also collected subjective data through questionnaires.

> 🖉 This is a good answer because the candidate shows excellent knowledge of fear arousal and the Leventhal et al. study and also good understanding of the wider psychological issues surrounding the fear-arousal technique. By the end of the answer it is clear what issues he/she will bring to their part (b) answer. In relation to the mark scheme, the description of the study itself is accurate, relevant, coherent and detailed. The candidate has made correct *and* comprehensive use of psychological terminology. The quality of the answer is evident. The answer is organised and it is grammatically correct with no spelling errors. This answer would achieve top band 9–10 marks.

(b) Effectiveness means 'does it work?' There are many debates to be raised regarding the effectiveness of this health promotion technique. The first one is whether a strong fear arousal is more effective than a moderate or mild one. The Leventhal study suggested that it is and this is confirmed by a study by Thornton et al. in 2000. However Janis and Feshback found that lower arousal was more effective. But it depends on what is being promoted. The Leventhal study was on smokers, the Janis study on oral hygiene and the Thornton study on speeding drivers. So just because one study claims a level of fear is effective, this does not mean that it is effective for every health behaviour that we promote. And related to this is the limited sample on which a study is based. Often students are used, the numbers of participants are limited and a study is only done in one country. But we can generalise to a certain extent because the Leventhal study was done in the USA, the Cowpat study on chip pans in the UK and the Thornton study in Australia and they all found that fear arousal worked.

A related issue is ethics. It could be argued that a strong fear arousal is not effective if it is unethical, but there is also the argument that if someone will give up smoking then the more they are scared, the more likely they are to give up. But, there are other techniques that are often used, such as providing information to people, which have also shown to be effective.

Another issue is whether using fear arousal in a snapshot study can be said to be effective. In the Leventhal study if smokers say they will give up smoking as they walk out of the lab then it is claimed that the technique is effective. But the participants might just be saying they will give up. A longitudinal study is needed to judge true effectiveness. If the smokers were asked a week later or a month later, then if they had truly given up then the technique could be said to be effective. This was confirmed by the Cowpat chip pan study where the effectiveness of the campaign wore off during the weeks after the campaign.

Another issue to judge effectiveness is whether the judgement is based on subjective or objective data. In the Leventhal study the smokers said they would give up smoking on a questionnaire. But they might have been doing this to please the experimenters (demand characteristics) or they might just have been giving socially desirable answers. This does not make something effective. Similarly, if they were to be given a questionnaire after a month then effectiveness could still not be judged. If an objective measure were to be used then there would be hard, scientific evidence, which is much better. So the smokers could have been given a breath or saliva sample to objectively judge whether they had been smoking or not, and if they had not, then it could be said that the programme was effective. Another issue is that people change their minds. The smokers might have wanted to give up as they left the study, but habits and lifestyles are very hard to change.

🖉 This is a superb answer. There are many evaluative points that cover a range of issues. Each point is dealt with effectively before the candidate moves on to the next. The answer is organised and it is balanced and well developed. The use of psychological terminology is impressive and the candidate clearly understands what he/she is writing. The use of examples is wide-ranging and each shows a good understanding of the area of health promotion. The candidate actually addresses the question — the *effectiveness* of health-promotion techniques — by discussing how effectiveness can be determined. This is an impressive answer that would achieve top band (12–15) marks and would be near the top end of that band.

Healthy living: adherence

(a) Describe one reason why people do not adhere to medical requests. (10 marks)

(b) Discuss the problems psychologists might have when carrying out studies on adherence to medical requests. (15 marks)

> 🖉 This question covers the *Healthy living* section of the specification: sub-section *Features of adherence to medical regimes and supporting evidence*, specifically reasons for non-adherence: cognitive rational non-adherence. The exemplar study is Bulpitt, but any appropriate study can be credited. Question part (a) is AO1, knowledge and understanding. Question part (b) can include any relevant problem that is related to adherence, which is AO2.

■ ■ ■

Answer to question 2: candidate A

(a) One reason for non-adherence to medical requests is that patients believe that it is not in their interests to take their medicine. This was shown in a study by Bulpitt (1988). The study was done on patients with high blood pressure and they were taking a new drug that had come onto the market. Although the drug worked in some respects, it caused them many problems and side effects in other areas. For example, the male patients were assessed in relation to headaches, depression, sleepiness, impotence and problems with ejaculation. Compared to before they started taking the drug, their headaches went down and so did their depression. Their level of sleepiness stayed the same, but they had increased problems with impotence and ejaculation. As a result, many of the men stopped taking the drug, because they had a rational reason for their non-adherence.

> 🖉 The Bulpitt study is named on the specification, so this is a relevant study to write about. This answer is generally accurate and it has made some use of psychological terminology. While the description of the study is generally accurate, it is more of a summary and the answer isn't particularly detailed. For instance, there is little elaboration and there are no additional examples given. The candidate doesn't add any detail about the Bulpitt study in relation to the method, sample, whether it is snapshot or longitudinal, whether the data are qualitative or quantitative, or any other relevant use of psychological terms and concepts. Nevertheless, the candidate does understand how this is a study of rational non-adherence. The answer is logically structured and grammar and spelling are good. This answer would be in the middle of the 6–8 mark band.

(b) The difficulties in carrying out studies into patient adherence are that patients are all different and they all have different interactions with the doctor and even doctors will not produce medical advice in the same way as say another doctor. This makes it difficult to say that patient adherence can be looked at on the same

question

level for example some patients adhere to medical advice better than others or maybe to parts of it i.e. taking pills for a short while but if told to give up smoking, do not wish to do so while if others are told to give up smoking because of health implications they do so.

Another difficulty is the differences between age and gender which brings up the issue of individual differences.

Ethics also needs to be taken into consideration as asking about people's health and what they do could be personal and if it is in a doctor's waiting room they may feel intimidated or obliged to do it in order to receive medical consultation. Asking questions on if they are on medication could be private and could cause stress.

Another issue is that self-reports could be subjective or show demand characteristics as the patient may know what is required of them. Diaries on patient adherence would be useful but this again may cause demand characteristics as they may feel they have to adhere to the medical advice. Individuals have different perspectives on adherence and medical advice.

📝 This is a below-average answer. The candidate makes a number of evaluative points but these are limited and often not related directly to the question. For example, the point about ethics is rather naive: clearly, any participant will give full informed consent and will not be asked to discuss personal data in a waiting room. However, there are a number of relevant points and this answer is better than a bottom band 1–3 mark answer. That said, it is not good enough to achieve either of the top two bands. The answer's argument is limited, as are its evaluation points. There are some valid conclusions and there is some understanding. The quality of grammar is poor. Overall, this would score in the 4–7 mark band, achieving less than half of the available marks.

■ ▨ ■

Answer to question 2: candidate B

(a) One reason why people may not adhere to medical requests is that they do not like the style of the medical practitioner. Studies have shown that if the practitioner exhibits a particular style, such as one that is patient-centred, and the patient prefers a practitioner-centred approach, then the patient may not be satisfied and then not adhere to the medical request given by the practitioner. One study that looked into how practitioners interact with their patients is the study conducted by Savage and Armstrong in 1990. They investigated whether a practitioner's consulting style had an effect on patient satisfaction. Their research was conducted over 4 months in a group practice in an inner city area of London. Four patients belonging to each doctor were randomly selected for the study. Patients were selected if they were aged 18–75 years, had no life-threatening condition, if they were not attending for administrative reasons and if the GP involved considered that they would not be upset by the project. This is an example of a snapshot study as only one piece of research was done on each patient for around 10–15 minutes. Overall 200 patients completed all assessments and were included in the data analysis. When a patient entered the consulting room, they were greeted and asked to describe their problem. When this was completed the GP then turned over a card to determine the appropriate style of consultation. The styles were either a sharing consulting style (patient-centred) or a directive consulting style (doctor-centred). Each consultation was recorded and assessed. All the participants were asked to complete a questionnaire immediately after the consultation and after a week. It was found that a directive consulting style produced higher levels of satisfaction in the patients so they were likely to have higher levels of adherence. The patient preference for a particular style is a perfect example of a rational reason for their behaviour.

> The Savage and Armstrong study isn't one that would immediately come to mind for an example of rational non-adherence, but the candidate makes it relevant and so it will receive just as much credit as if the Bulpitt study was described.
>
> The candidate has made correct and comprehensive use of psychological terminology. The description of the study is accurate, coherent and it is detailed. Remember that you have only approximately 8 minutes to write this answer. Particularly good is where the candidate has elaborated on the study. First, the candidate has made the study relevant to the question and second there are instances of understanding — for instance, where the snapshot study is mentioned. The answer is competently structured and organised and there are no spelling or grammar errors. This answer would be in the 9–10 mark band.

(b) There are many problems psychologists have when studying adherence. It is very difficult to find a representative sample. This is because, due to ethical reasons such as privacy and confidentiality, the patient volunteer has to be involved in the study. The likelihood is that people who do not adhere to medical advice are not likely to volunteer to take part in the study. This was shown in a study by Riekart and Drotar when they studied diabetics. Therefore, the rates of adherence found as a result of the study do not generalise to a majority population.

Another problem with adherence studies is that there are many methodological problems because it is difficult to measure. For example, when some people consider themselves to be complying with medical advice they may not actually be following all of the instructions, just most of them, so they are not actually adhering correctly even though they say they are. Adherence is also very difficult to measure. There are objective and subjective approaches to measuring adherence. The subjective approaches include asking the patient to judge their own adherence or asking the doctor to judge their patient's compliance. As these subjective approaches and their accuracy and reliability is based on the person telling the truth, or understanding what is actually meant by complete adherence, the answers that they give cannot be the only way of measuring it.

question

To increase the reliability of the results objective measures can also be used, however there are problems with this approach as well. For example, objective measures include using medication dispensers and biochemical measures such as blood tests and urine tests. Although biochemical techniques should be reliable because they are scientific, they are low in validity and cannot be used for adherence to certain medications, they cannot be used if the medical advice involves adopting a healthy behaviour or stopping an unhealthy behaviour.

To make measuring adherence as accurate as possible the subjective and objective approaches should be used together. There are also very many other problems when carrying out studies on adherence for example, problems when working with children and demand characteristics which may result from the situation e.g. the fact that the doctor is an authoritative figure may cause some patients to exaggerate their adherence.

This is a good answer for a number of reasons. The candidate considers a range of different problems, provides relevant examples, uses appropriate terminology and makes effective comments. The answer is quite detailed too. On the negative side, the answer isn't always clear in exactly what point is being made; there is only one example quoted; terms are not explained (such as 'reliability') and grammar and punctuation are poor in places. The answer has some evaluative points covering a range of issues, rather than many evaluative points. It is well organised but lacks balance or development. Use of examples is good rather than effective. In relation to the mark scheme, despite the negatives, this is a good answer and would be in one of the top two mark bands. Overall, this answer would be placed in the 8–11 mark band.

Q3

Stress: managing stress

(a) Describe one technique for managing stress. (10 marks)

(b) Evaluate the success of stress management programmes. (15 marks)

> This question covers the *Stress* section of the specification: sub-section *Techniques for managing stress and supporting evidence*. Three approaches are included: cognitive, behavioural and social. There are exemplars for each but any appropriate study can be credited. Question part (a) is AO1, knowledge and understanding. Question part (b) is AO2 and can include any relevant point to assess the success of stress management programmes.

■ ■ ■

Answer to question 3: candidate A

(a) A technique used to manage stress is the cognitive one of imagery. This involves imagining yourself in a safe, warm environment. I would imagine myself on the beach whereas others may imagine theirself somewhere else. The idea is to relax and focus on what your imagining. This should be done regularly for short periods of time. In a warm and quiet place to start with until you have got the hang of it. Eventually you will be able to do this wherever you are or whatever you are doing and not only when you start to feel stressed.

> The candidate has chosen an appropriate stress-management technique because imagery is an appropriate cognitive technique for managing stress. He/she clearly understands what imagery involves: it is cognitive rather than behavioural or social (or biological) and it can be applied anywhere. However, the answer is very general and no specific piece of psychological research is quoted. Psychological terminology is sparse, or basic at best. Description is limited and lacks detail, but it is generally accurate. Spelling and grammar are poor. This answer would achieve a mark at the bottom of the 3–5 mark band, scoring 3 marks out of the available 10.

(b) One problem in measuring the effectiveness of stress management programmes is that you can never be sure how stressed people are. As in self-report methods participants have a tendency to be hypochondriacs and exaggerate their stress levels. There are physiological tests which can be carried out to look at the symptoms of stress e.g. blood pressure, heart rate, temperature. However, these do not tell us the reasons for the stress, how long it has been going on, and how severe it is. So it is therefore hard to tell how well stress management programmes are working. You can't truly rely on self-report measures and physiological measures as they don't give a full enough picture. One way stress management programmes could be looked at to see how effective they are is through observational methods. However, it would be hard to observe certain behaviours linked to stress, without the patient seeing you. It would also be unethical to be watching people without their consent. However, if the patient was informed this could lead to demand characteristics. This may also put the patient under stress which could cause results to be wrong. Also in any observation observer bias has to be taken into account. So if we don't know how stressed someone is in the first place it is very difficult to say how effective their stress management programme has been. The only person that could really tell us is the patient and they may exaggerate or underestimate the stress.

> The candidate takes the view that the success of any stress-management programme must be measured in some way and that there are a number of difficulties in this. The candidate then runs through a range of different ways in which stress can be measured: physiological tests, self-report measures and observation. Some basic advantages and disadvantages of each of these are presented. While the candidate makes the point about measurement well, the answer really consists of just one point with quite a lot of elaboration. There are examples, but these amount to nothing more than 'e.g. blood pressure' rather than examples from actual studies. What is really needed is a more detailed look at the success of stress-management programmes from various angles. Although the candidate would score lower marks for a limited range of evaluation points, there is elaboration that is related to the context of the question. More credit can be given because there are valid conclusions with regard to the method, but then it can be argued that the comments about methods are too general and are not sufficiently focused on the question itself. This answer does not neatly fit into any band of the mark scheme, but overall it would be placed in the 4–7 mark band, scoring at the bottom end of that mark range.

■ ■ ■

Answer to question 3: candidate B

(a) One technique used to manage stress is stress inoculation. This technique was outlined and tested in a study by Meichenbaum (1975). It is a form of cognitive therapy and the technique involves preparing people for stressful situations by taking part in activities and so learning to use positive stress responses. The first part of stress inoculation is conceptualisation. This involves the subject and the teacher talking about previous stress responses to learn about how they react to stressors and what they may have been doing wrong. The second part is skill acquisition. This involves the teacher presenting appropriate ways to deal with stress, should a stressful situation occur. Such techniques involve basic behavioural and cognitive skills such as relaxation techniques. The third and final part of stress inoculation is when the teacher guides the subject through a series of progressively more stressful situations, where the subject practises his or her appropriate stress responses. The idea is that when a real-life situation occurs, the subject will be able to apply what they have learned and be able to cope and manage stress.

e This candidate has provided an excellent summary of the stress inoculation technique outlined by Meichenbaum. He/she describes correctly the three stages and clearly understands what the technique involves. For the 8 minutes available in which to write an answer, this candidate has provided a concise summary. In terms of marks, the answer shows competent use of terminology. Description of the technique is accurate, coherent and reasonably detailed. There is some elaboration, but this could be better. The structure of the answer is logical and spelling and grammar are good. This answer would score 8 marks out of the available 10. Note that this candidate has balanced the amount of time spent on question part (a) appropriately compared to the amount of time spent on the answer to question part (b).

(b) It is difficult to measure the success of stress management programmes because to do so, psychologists would have to either be present when the subject is going through stressful situations, to measure the stress responses, or they would have to engineer false situations. Either way, the way the subject responded would lack ecological validity, especially in the laboratory, so the results could perhaps not be replicated in real life. The presence of a psychologist would affect the way the person behaved, as they may deliberately behave in a certain way to impress the psychologist, and react in a completely different way in private. The subject themselves could report whether the programme had been a success, either by an actual self-report or via a questionnaire. This would measure coping in real environments, but again the subject may want to seem as if they are complying with social norms, or may be deliberately non-compliant, by saying that the programme either was or wasn't effective, when it may not be true. Rather than subjective measures, a more objective way of measuring stress is needed. Perhaps the subject should have regular blood pressure tests because stress is also physio-logical and not just cognitive and if blood pressure is reduced then this would show that the programme had been successful. If this were done over time it would be even better. Another issue is whether what had been learned in the Meichenbaum programme could be generalised to every situation or whether it applies only to certain stressors. For example, would the techniques apply to daily hassles being the cause of stress or just to a work based environment. But as it is a cognitive technique then it should generalise.

e This a competent answer written by a candidate who shows good understanding of both the topic area in question and appropriate issues and methods in psychology, and how to apply this knowledge to the mark scheme. The candidate presents a number of issues to assess success: ecological validity, subjective and objective measures and the ability to generalise. There is also an awareness of the different causes and measures of stress that stress is both physiological and cognitive. Overall, this is an impressive answer. In terms of marks, there is a range of evaluative points covering a range of issues. The answer is balanced and related to the question. There is a good use of examples and the candidate shows both analysis and understanding. This answer would appear in the top mark band.

Dysfunctional behaviour: explanations

(a) Describe one explanation for dysfunctional behaviour. (10 marks)

(b) Evaluate explanations for dysfunctional behaviours. (15 marks)

> This question covers the *Dysfunctional behaviour* section of the specification: sub-section *Explanations of dysfunctional behaviour*; three bullet points appear here along with exemplars. Question part (a) is AO1, knowledge and understanding. Question part (b) uses evaluation of explanations for dysfunctional behaviour to assess AO2: application of knowledge and understanding.

■ ■ ■

Answer to question 4: candidate A

(a) Models of abnormality are paradigms used to explain abnormal behaviour and actions with reference to particular theories. There are basically five theories of abnormality. The biological or physiological model of abnormality lays emphasis on the fact that abnormality is caused by a malfunction in the brain, some sort of problem in the hormonal system or because of factors such as chromosome mutation and genes. The psychological theories of abnormality encompass a psychodynamic view, a behavioural view, a cognitive view and a socio-cultural view. The psychodynamic view has been forwarded by Freud. In this paradigm, it is said that all psychological problems occur when the ego is unable to control the id and the superego. Factors that are underlying in the subconscious mind which have not been resolved cause a person to incur psychological problems. The cognitive model on the other hand, emphasises the mind as being incapable of allocating issues correctly or in a manner that is prevalent in most humans. This included problems such as erroneous thinking. However, the behavioural view implies that all of what humans do is learnt and it is behaviour which when corrected by means of either classical conditioning or operant conditioning, will result in overcoming or reducing this abnormality.

> This candidate has not answered the question set. As the candidate correctly states, there are a number of different explanations of dysfunctional behaviour, but this does not mean they should all be included in an answer. First, the question only asks for one explanation and so any more would not receive credit. Second, the specification states that three explanations need to be covered: biological, behavioural and cognitive. The specification does not include the psychodynamic approach. To answer the question set, the candidate only writes a few lines that can be credited and, regardless of the three explanations offered, the answer is so brief that it would only achieve bottom band marks (1–3).

(b) No model is without flaw as they are all devised with particular theories in mind which are widely recognised and accepted; however, the various models of abnormality are subjective to the sort of abnormality in focus. The physiological model suggests that abnormality is of a physical nature, however, continuous research has shown that genetic trends may be very low in monozygote twins, and in family trees, but for some illnesses this may not be true, for example autism is 91% genetically based. A contrast to this is the behavioural model which suggests that abnormalities may be learnt and then also unlearnt. This was seen in the ever-so-famous case of the boy little Albert, in Watson's study. The psychologists were able to inhibit a phobia of white things in the boy by using Pavlov's classical conditioning approach. As to this, it is a matter of fact that most armed personnel services use this method to train their recruits. Still, operative conditioning has been used in reinforcing positive or negative sanctions in order for a person to strive for a reward and hence change their behaviour. This approach has been used for depression as well as phobias. Rational emotive behavioural therapy is also constantly used to treat various abnormalities. The cognitive model, furthermore, attempts to strengthen a person's perception and thinking. In this matter, it works towards proving that erroneous thought processes when corrected will lead to a positive result and will encounter and treat the psychological problem inevitably. Beck advocates this model. However, Freud, without much consistent support for his work, advocates the use of therapy in which the subject is able to talk through whatever is in their subconscious mind. In this way, dreams and thought processes will be interpreted in the light of past experiences so as to shed light on the exact cause of the problem. As most of Freud's work is based on case studies a number of issues with regards to his theory have been raised. Most models of abnormality work better if multiple facets are applied rather than just focusing on one model. This is true for most diagnosis, explanation and treatment. It has been researched time and time again, with respect to problems such as ADHD, autism, phobias, obsessive-compulsive disorder, depression and the likes of it; and the conclusion still stands that no single explanation is good enough in isolation and neither is any one treatment.

The candidate knows quite a lot about various explanations of dysfunctional behaviour and has taken the opportunity to describe them here. There is an outline of the genetic explanation followed by a description of the behavioural explanation with details of the little Albert study, followed by Pavlov. The candidate then moves on to describe rational emotive therapy and the work of Beck. Finally, Freud is introduced. The crucial point is that the candidate is *describing* various explanations and although what is written shows a good understanding of a wide range of explanations, there needs to be much more evaluation. To answer a question like this perhaps the best approach would be to compare and contrast explanations. In terms of marks, this answer would be placed in the 4–7 mark band.

Answer to question 4: candidate B

(a) In the study of abnormal psychology there are five main models: the medical (or biological), the behavioural, the cognitive, the psychodynamic and the humanistic. In this answer I will outline the behavioural model. The behavioural model explains psychological disorders as being 'maladaptive behaviours' that are taken on by patients and used in this way as 'adaptive behaviours'. Hence, the behavioural model focuses on the present behaviour of the patients and tends to observe their 'environment' to gain an understanding about the development of these disorders. Maladaptive behaviours are learned according to BF Skinner through operant conditioning. Skinner uses the terms 'reinforcers' to describe anything that causes the frequency of a particular behaviour to increase. Positive reinforcers provide a positive stimulus and cause an increase in frequency of a particular behaviour, whereas negative reinforcers cause the frequency of a behaviour to increase by removing the pleasant stimulus. 'Punishers' is the term used to define an act that is used to decrease the frequency of a behaviour. Hence, Skinner believes that an inappropriate form of reinforcement used on a person can cause psychological disorders such as phobias. Another behavioural explanation for psychological disorders is that of 'classical conditioning'. In this, a stimulus that usually triggers a response from a person normally (unconditional response stimulus) is repeatedly paired with a neutral stimulus that usually does not trigger a response. Over time, even when the previously neutral stimulus is shown or presented without the unconditional response stimulus, it will start receiving a response. It has now been turned into a 'conditional stimulus'. Using classical conditioning even pathological fear can be instilled in a person. Hence, a psychological disorder can be seen as a neutral stimulus that when repeatedly paired with an unconditional stimulus, turns into a conditional stimulus. This theory can be very effective in explaining phobias such as agoraphobia.

    This is a really good answer. The candidate understands that there are a number of different approaches, and suggests that he or she knows about all five, but has focused on just one, as the question requests. The candidate knows that the behavioural model is based on both classical and operant conditioning and makes a clear distinction between the two. The description of maladaptive behaviours is good, and the candidate uses many appropriate jargon terms. Disappointingly, an example of dysfunctional behaviour only appears at the end of the paragraph. The description of operant conditioning is also quite good and appropriate jargon terms are used by the candidate. Yet again, an example of a dysfunctional behaviour only appears at the end of the paragraph. The answer could have been improved if the description had more clarity and if an example of a dysfunctional behaviour appeared throughout the answer. Despite a number of weaknesses, there are strengths, and this answer would score in the 6–8 mark band.

(b) The behavioural model is criticised on the grounds that it tends to get highly reductionist at times particularly by supporters of the psychodynamic model. But then the biological model is also reductionist. The main criticism is that the behavioural model fails to take into account past experiences that psychological patients tend to go through, and focusing only on the present. Supporters of Freud will argue that focusing only on the present will not deal with the 'unresolved conflicts' in the patient's mind, so that even if one psychological disorder is cured, these conflicts will rise in the form of another disorder. However, the behavioural model has based most of its theories on extensive lab experiments which means that the theories are based on reliable data. However, lab experiments are again conducted mainly on animals, so results cannot be applied to humans, and to real life in general. The medical model is also reductionist and a disadvantage of this model is that it tends to label people as 'sick' and doctors tend to make type 1 errors rather than type 2 errors, i.e. labelling a healthy person as sick, rather than a sick person as healthy. Hence the diagnoses made from the medical model are unethical and cannot be trusted fully. Given that, the behavioural model is strictly ethical, because it tends to focus on a person's adaptive and maladaptive behaviours rather than labelling a person as sick or insane.

The candidate writes more for part (a) than for part (b), nearly 70 words more, despite there being more available marks for part (b): 10 marks in total for part (a) and 15 marks for part (b). The candidate begins by considering reductionism, which is an appropriate evaluation point. However, there is no explanation of what this is, and although the candidate makes correct comments in relation to both the psychodynamic and biological explanations there is no elaboration at all. The candidate makes another evaluative point about past experiences and compares the behavioural explanation with the psychodynamic. Note that the psychodynamic explanation does not appear on the specification, so including it in an answer shows evidence of work beyond the specification. However, the point is brief with no elaboration. The candidate then makes a number of poor assertions. The original behaviourist experiments may have involved animals (Pavlov and dogs; Skinner and pigeons) but the approach has shown numerous human examples, beginning with little Albert, for example. Further, there is the assertion that doctors make type 1 errors, which is not the case. Overall, the answer has a number of evaluative comments, covering a limited range of issues. These comments are related to the context of the question, but have no elaboration. There are valid conclusions, but also some that are not valid. This answer would be placed in the middle band mark range of 4–7 marks.

Disorders: characteristics and causes

(a) Describe the characteristics and causes for one disorder. (10 marks)

(b) Review causes for one disorder. (15 marks)

This question covers the *Disorders* section of the specification, which has two sub-sections: *Characteristics of disorders* and *Explanations of one disorder*. Three bullet points appear here, allowing candidates to choose either an affective (e.g. bipolar disorder) anxiety based (such as a phobia) or psychotic (such as schizophrenia) disorder. Question part (a) requires two main parts and is AO1, knowledge and understanding. Question part (b) asks for a review of causes for a disorder, to assess AO2, and logically this will be the same disorder as was described in part (a).

■ ■ ■

Answer to question 5: candidate A

(a) Schizophrenia is termed as splitting of various functions of the brain. Symptoms of schizophrenia are as follows: a schizophrenic person experiences hallucinations which are responses which are heard in the absence of stimuli. These are mainly auditory. The schizophrenic hears voices commenting in his/her head, sometimes voices arguing or telling the schizophrenic what to do. These hallucinations take place at such a high frequency that normal functioning is impaired. Furthermore a schizophrenic experiences delusions which are misconceptions about the world and reality and feeling the world is unreal. Delusions are mainly persecutory i.e. feeling that the whole world is plotting against you. Even your friends are among the plotters and your family cannot convince you that this isn't true.

There are a number of explanations for the development of schizophrenia. The medical or biological explanation has two parts: the chemical and the genetic. The medical states that overproduction of neurotransmitter dopamine leads to development of this disorder. This was found as drugs that have an effect on symptoms decrease dopamine levels. Genes show that a person can be predisposed to having schizophrenia, and whether the person develops this disorder depends on the environment. Research has shown that closest family or relatives of schizophrenics have 10% more chance of developing schizophrenia while only 1% with normal relatives are at risk. Twin studies have shown that if one identical twin has this disorder, so will the other, which is not the case for fraternal twins.

This candidate addresses each aspect of this question specifically and begins by describing the characteristics of one disorder — schizophrenia. He/she then describes one cause for schizophrenia (the biological model), specifically that the cause is attributable to genes. While the answer is not perfect, it would score high marks. The candidate could have mentioned the different types of schizophrenia (e.g. catatonic or disorganised) and could have included specific studies (e.g. Gottesman and Shields, 1972 or Oruc et al. 1998) on the genetic relationship to schizophrenia. Despite these weaknesses this answer would score in the 6–8 mark band, with a final mark of **7 out of 10**.

(b) Dear Examiner, I spent quite a lot of time planning my part (a) answer and writing it and so I now have very little time to write my part (b). I hope you will be sympathetic and mark my notes kindly. I would have included:

- Alternative explanations for schizophrenia such as the chemical hypothesis. I would consider non-biological explanations such as...

This candidate is typical of many who do not plan their time and then lose marks because they run out of time. A successful candidate will spend time on each question that equates to the marks allocated. For OCR psychology papers, the recommended time allocations are 8 minutes for question part (a) and 14 minutes for question part (b).

Examiners must mark what is written, that is not crossed out, including notes. However, there is no point in writing a 'Dear Examiner' letter because this gets no sympathy whatsoever. For the notes of this candidate, the 'chemical hypothesis' is a legitimate alternative to the genetic explanation and there is understanding that there are non-biological explanations, although the candidate does not say what they are. This answer would score **1 mark out of the 15 available**.

■ ■ ■

Answer to question 5: candidate B

(a) One disorder is a phobia. According to the behaviourists all behaviours are learned and so they believe that fears and phobias are also learned. It all began with Pavlov (1890), who classically conditioned a dog to salivate at the sound of a bell. Before conditioning the UCS is food and the UCR is salivation. During conditioning the UCS (food) is paired with the CS (the bell). Until this association is formed the dog will still salivate because of the food. When the dog has been conditioned, then the CS (the bell) will cause the CR to happen, which is the dog salivating. There are all sorts of other terms here, like stimulus generalisation and discrimination, but there is no time to describe them. Watson picked up on Pavlov's idea and with Raynor (1920) he classically conditioned little Albert to be scared of a white rat. Lots of people get muddled with white animals, but it was a rat (according to YouTube video). Watson used exactly the same formula as Pavlov: UCS > UCR; UCS + CS > UCR; CS > CR. In real-life it doesn't quite work like this as people can be conditioned without really knowing it, like the man who had a phobia of a No.5 bus because that was the bus he caught when he went to have his teeth taken out when he was young.

question

The characteristics of a phobia are as follows: they only happen if people come into contact with the object they have been conditioned to respond to and when this happens they have a major anxiety attack. It involves feelings of nervousness and that the person can't cope. It has physiological reactions such as increased heart rate, sweating, muscle tension and rapid breathing.

> This candidate has answered the question well, providing good answers for both the cause and the characteristics. The description of Pavlov's work is concise and all the terminology, UCS, CR etc. all correct. The description of Watson's work is also accurate, although quoting a YouTube video doesn't really count as evidence. The anecdotal example of the No. 5 bus doesn't have a reference for it, but at least it shows that the candidate understands the conditioning process. The characteristics of a phobia are fine and the candidate has chosen to do this in a generalised way rather than explain it through a specific phobia. This is a very good answer in the time allowed and would score in the top mark band.

(b) By reviewing the causes I think the examiner means to look at various other causes for anxiety disorders to evaluate the behaviourist explanation. Firstly there are problems with the behaviourist approach. It assumes that all behaviour is learned when this might not be the case. Some behaviours might be inherited and this is the nature–nurture debate. The behaviourist explanation is also reductionist because it reduces the whole process of anxiety and all other behaviours to a simple formula. Perhaps our behaviour is much more complex than this and the reductionist view is false. But, in their favour, behaviourists believe that they should only study observable behaviour and that makes their approach scientific, unlike other approaches. Another approach, or explanation for anxiety is the psychoanalytic one, by Freud. He believes that the id is selfish and wants immediate gratification. But the ego and superego put it in check. The id doesn't like it and this conflict between the three causes anxiety. The anxiety is pushed onto some other object and the person has a phobia. The case study of Little Hans showed this in his phobia of horses. This was a case study, where we can't generalise and it isn't scientific. It is deterministic because the cause of anxiety is said to be the unconscious mind. In many ways this is totally different from the behaviorist explanation. Another explanation is the cognitive one. Beck says that we have schemas for everything including anxiety and our negative thoughts cause us anxiety and depression. Di Nardo has the best work because Di Nardo says that the behaviourist explanation isn't enough. People don't just associate bad experiences with dogs and have a phobia. Some do and some don't, so why? Di Nardo says it depends on whether people expect to be hurt by a dog and whether they interpret the event as being traumatic. So this goes beyond the simple behaviourist explanation. Although cognitive behaviour is the modern approach the cognitive approach itself has the problem of subject matter and like Freud, how can people's thoughts be studied. Overall, there are different explanations for phobias, and maybe one day a psychologist will propose a theory that will bring everything together into one theory.

This is an excellent answer. The candidate clearly understands a number of explanations for anxiety and phobias and has outlined each accurately and concisely. There are valid conclusions that effectively summarise. He/she also refers to quite a number of issues. There are comments about methodology (observations and case studies) and although the candidate could have considered these in more detail, appropriate comments are made in relation to the explanation being considered. The issues of reductionism, determinism and nature–nurture are also raised. Again, this is done briefly, but the candidate has gone for breadth rather than depth and clearly understands these issues. A further strength is that the candidate hasn't just listed alternative explanations, or just described each. Rather, he/she has compared and contrasted throughout. This answer would score in the highest mark band.